Lead Me

D0071504

"This transparent and inspiring book verbalized so many things I have felt but have never talked about—the tension between work and family, marriage challenges, family life, anxiety, and hearing a call to 'come home.' It put a lump in my throat and made me laugh out loud (many times!). Matt has challenged me to be not just a man of polished presentations and good intentions but a man of authenticity and action. This intimate and exposed look into Matt's and Sarah's personal, professional, and spiritual lives gives me the courage and hope I need to be the man, the husband, and the father I've always wanted to be for my wife and kids."

—KIRK CAMERON, television and film actor and producer

"A gritty, authentic read about a courageous man who chose to step up and double down on loving and leading his wife and family spiritually. This is an epic book that every man, married or single, should read and have for his journey of becoming the man God created him to be. Buy an extra copy for a friend . . . We all need the kind of practical encouragement that Matt brings."

—DR. DENNIS RAINEY, cofounder of FamilyLife

"I grew up being inspired by the honesty of Matt Hammitt and Sanctus Real's lyrics. Their words and melodies met me in places of anxiety and doubt, while leading me back into the arms of Jesus above all else. At its core, this book carries the messages of the music we all love dearly. The transparency in Matt's (and Sarah's) storytelling is captivating as both a reader and a longtime fan turned friend. And as first-time parents, my husband and I have been encouraged and challenged by *Lead Me* to keep Christ at the forefront with every step we take for our marriage and family."

— JAMIE GRACE, Grammy-nominated singer-songwriter

"I've enjoyed Matt's friendship for many years, and I'm grateful that he's sharing his story with great honesty and transparency. The valleys in life can produce character and perseverance, and you'll be challenged and encouraged by the character that's on display throughout this book."

—LUKE SMALLBONE, for King & Country

"Reading this book unlocked such a beautiful picture of a man choosing his family—embracing that no mission, platform, or opportunity is more important than the mission at home. It has reminded me as a husband and father not to miss the most important responsibility that God trusted to me alone. This story is powerful and will move you to tears and to action."

—ANDREW ERWIN, filmmaker, *I Can Only Imagine*

"I've always appreciated Matt's willingness to bare his soul—for years in Sanctus Real's music and now in his new book, *Lead Me*. He uses how God has comforted and challenged him in the past to encourage and comfort others in their own journeys, and that's exactly what the Bible encourages us to do."

—SCOTT SMITH, on-air personality at K-LOVE Radio

"Matt does a brilliant job of pointing men back to the real hero of our families . . . Jesus."

—JERRAD LOPES, founder of Dad Tired

LEAD ME

FINDING COURAGE TO FIGHT FOR
YOUR MARRIAGE, CHILDREN, AND FAITH

MATT HAMMITT

FOREWORD BY BART MILLARD

MULTNOMAH

Lead Me

Trade Paperback ISBN 978-0-525-65331-8
eBook ISBN 978-0-525-65332-5

Copyright © 2020 by Matt Hammitt

Cover design by Kristopher K. Orr
Cover photograph by David Molnar

Published in the United States by Multnomah, an imprint of Random House, a division of Penguin Random House LLC.

Multnomah® and its mountain colophon are registered trademarks of Penguin Random House LLC.

The Cataloging-in-Publication Data is on file with the Library of Congress.

Printed in the United States of America
2020—First Edition

10 9 8 7 6 5 4 3 2 1

*For the one who hopes to find meaning at
the end of their hard story.
Sarah, our struggles will not be wasted.*

Contents

Father, Show Me the Way

Foreword

I know how hard it can be to wear a happy face when you're hurting inside. For over twenty years, I've been telling some difficult parts of my story from the stage, through songs, and most recently on the big screen. Maybe you've heard how I grew up in a small town in Texas, with an abusive father behind closed doors. I smile as I tell how God's grace turned him into the dad I'd always wanted before he died. That same grace continues to transform me too.

But even when I'm smiling, I feel the reality of loss, the sting of my failures, and the ever-present struggle to keep embracing what I know— that God loves me just as I am.

Truth is, there was a time I was so lost in the painful parts of childhood that I was missing out on the most important parts of adulthood. I had let the busyness of my career distract me from my responsibilities at home, and my identity was wrapped up in the highs and lows of MercyMe. Kingdom work had become the villain that was stealing my heart from Shannon and the kids. The very thing I thought was noble was slowly chipping away at my family.

It's a scary thing to stop and look in the mirror at the parts of yourself you'd rather not see. It took my wife, Shannon, going to counseling and then successfully and lovingly luring me along with her to start my path to healing. To start seeing the whole picture of who I was, who I am, and who God is shaping me to be.

Around the time I first heard Matt singing "Lead Me" about his shortcomings as a husband and father, I found myself standing face to face with my own. It's a hard battle when your children are looking at you saying, "Daddy, you're never home." I told the band that something had to change—that God isn't a God of chaos and that family has to win every time. We cut our tour schedule in half, started exercising the word *no,* and began taking real steps in the process of living what we claimed to believe about family being more important than our careers.

Shannon and I have spent the last couple of years growing in community with Matt and his wife, Sarah, along with a group of friends we call our village. Together we embrace the reality that marriage and life can be a real mess sometimes, doing our best to help carry one another's burdens as our own. We also share the challenges of parenting, including the grief of raising children with chronic illnesses. Along with sharing our pain, we experience the beauty of being loved, known, and accepted, not for what we give this village, but simply because we're a part of it. If that's not a piece of heaven on earth, then I don't know what is.

The journey is so hard when it feels hopeless. And hopelessness finds no better place to grow than when you're isolated. If you don't have good counsel or community, then I pray you seek it. But in the meantime, as you read this book, I want you to see that you're not alone. And I hope that God will give you an open heart to allow His redemption into your life and marriage. That you will find yourself ready to receive the healing that He has waiting for you.

—Bart Millard, MercyMe

Dear Reader

> But he said to me, "My grace is sufficient for you, for
> my power is made perfect in weakness." Therefore I
> will boast all the more gladly of my weaknesses, so
> that the power of Christ may rest upon me.
>
> —2 Corinthians 12:9

It's easier to judge a book by its cover than to wrestle with what's inside. That's probably why we spend so much time managing the covers of our own lives, trying to preserve the appearance that we're either normal or far more interesting than we really are. It gets messier the deeper you get into someone's life, and it's no small thing asking someone to go there with you.

Although this book is based on my story, the heart of it is an invitation to become who God has called you to be. And I believe the first step in that lifelong journey is coming to terms with the reality of who you are now versus who you are meant to become. Truth is hard, but to paraphrase King Solomon, reality wins in the end. Accepting yourself and others, scars and all, is a painful process. We were weak when we wanted to be strong, awkward when we longed to be cool, rejected when we hoped to be loved or at least recognized.

I could airbrush, cover up, and present a version of my life that's far more attractive than the truth. But who would that help? Real life comes with junk drawers and scary containers of leftovers you forgot were in the back of the fridge. It's not always pretty, but being honest about that stuff—that's what connects us. I don't know about you, but I can relate a lot more to people's screwups than their successes. If you really want my trust, don't just brag about your victories. Show me your scars.

Before we move on, I want to give you a couple of notes on how this book is structured. From time to time, you'll see some words from Sarah—as in Sarah, my wife. Her voice is so much a part of my life that to consider telling my story without including her seemed foolish. Her quotes are not accompanied by any commentary; rather, they're pauses where she steps into the story and says, "Okay, Matt. But this is how I saw it."

Finally, this book as a whole is divided into three main parts, made up of smaller sections. At the conclusion of each of the three main parts, you'll find six questions to reflect on. If you're reading through the book alone, you can respond to them on your own. But the questions are also useful in a group setting or if you're reading alongside a spouse or friend. Either way, I hope you'll take the time to consider the questions when you see them and answer honestly.

—Matt

Intro

The end of a matter is better than its beginning,

and patience is better than pride.

—ECCLESIASTES 7:8, NIV

I couldn't quit the band. I had a wife and four children depending on me to provide for them. There were mouths to feed, a mortgage to pay, and medical bills to sort out. How could I give up my sole source of income?

But my family needed more than financial provision. Something that another million streams of "Lead Me" couldn't give them. Sarah and the kids were hungry for me to provide for their emotional and spiritual needs, and I knew it was time for me to do more than just sing about it. I had to step up and be the man I was called to be, to move beyond my good intentions and take action as the spiritual leader of my family.

Throughout my career, I encouraged people to keep dreaming. Dreams are important, even biblical, but when your personal life is stressed to the point of collapsing, I think it's a sign that you may be chasing your dreams in the wrong direction.

I didn't have to give up crafting words and music for a living. I needed to find a new context in which to use my gifts, where I could be present and attentive *and* provide financial support for my wife and kids.

As much as I had leaned on it, a career in Christian music was not my provider. God was. I would have to trust and let go, believing that just as God brought my career with Sanctus Real at the proper time, He would provide each step of the way.

———

I planned to meet with my bandmates in person, but first I wrote a letter to pave the way.

> *Chris and Mark,*
>
> *I've wanted to talk with you both over the last few days, but I was concerned that I wouldn't remember all I needed to say in the moment. I felt that writing this letter would give me a sure opportunity to be clear and gracious with my words.*

How do you tell your closest friends that the life they've known for twenty years is over? The threads and layers of the life we shared were complex, woven together through time, love, brotherly struggles, and common accomplishments. Our bond was spiritual and emotional, and marked by our physical presence in each other's lives for almost twenty years. I did my very best.

> *As a husband, father, leader, and friend, I'm account-able for the things in my life that feel out of balance. I'm*

responsible to listen to God's voice and seek what He is trying
to teach me in my restlessness. My natural inclination is to
strive harder to fix things and to come up with solutions to
keep things moving forward at all costs. However, I think
Saint Augustine said it best when he wrote, "Lord . . . our
heart is unquiet until it rests in you."

I felt the weight fall from my chest as I wrote down the words I had
bottled up inside.

Obedience requires action, sacrifice, and hard conversa-
tions with people you love. Sometimes obedience requires
loss and causes questions that are difficult to answer, because
walking in faith can't be perfectly explained. It's not right
or fair to keep what God has been speaking to me hidden.
Everyone is searching for direction, and I need to speak out.
I've come to the place where I know, without a doubt, that
God is calling me to step out in faith and walk into a new
season, apart from the band.

There was more to the letter I wrote my bandmates, but most of all
I wanted to tell them that I loved them and that I was committed to
finishing strong.

———————

I boarded our tour bus late on a Thursday afternoon, knowing we had
a long ride through the night. I'd practiced the speech that would follow my letter a thousand times over in my head, hoping not to stutter,
praying the words would come out right.

The bus lounge was quiet, with only the hum of the engine to soothe my nerves. I had planned to call the band together but found myself alone with Chris and Mark, and one spilled word gave way to another. I explained how I'd felt spiritually restless for so long, how each time I performed "Lead Me," it burned in my chest that I was not that man. Those words I had written years earlier were still the cry of my heart.

The words I had rehearsed escaped me, and I began to speak from the heart. I let them know that I loved them as brothers, bandmates, friends. They were my family too. But my marriage was strained. The kids were growing up without me. Bowen had made it four years, but the reality was that his disease was progressing. Most of all, I knew that God was calling me to step into a new season of life.

The room became quiet. I took a long breath. "Guys, I'm done," I said. "It's hard to say, but . . . for good."

Mark got quiet, but Chris became understandably upset. Sanctus Real had started as just him and me, at Toledo Christian School. We were just kids.

As teenagers we answered God's call, and together we remained faithful to it through adversity. We had also shared the privilege of seeing lives touched and miracles happen through the mysterious power of ministry through music. But despite our successes, none of us could deny that life on the road had come at a great cost to our families. Ultimately, they would understand. But as with any life-altering change, this one would take time to accept.

Chasing Dreams

Early Years

To live by grace means to acknowledge my whole
life story, the light side and the dark. In admitting
my shadow side, I learn who I am and what God's
grace means.

—BRENNAN MANNING

They called me "The Barf King." Not the sort of cool nickname an
elementary school kid hopes for, certainly not "Ace" or "Lucky" or
something the fast, athletic kids get, like "Flash." Those would've been
good nicknames. But when you're a first grader with a nervous stomach
who upchucks in front of the water fountain while your classmates are
lined up to get a drink, Barf King it is.

I can't recall who blessed me with such a clever nickname. Maybe
the janitor whispered it around the halls as payback for all the times he
had to carry his push broom and sack of red sawdust to the scene of my
latest spew. Boy, that guy must've hated me.

I grew up in a neighborhood just northwest of downtown Toledo,
Ohio, only a mile away from the hospital where I was born. I rolled
with a small gang of neighborhood kids on the weekends but also had

a few friends at church, where the Hammitt family could be found most any time the doors were open.

Most of my early memories share the same location, Toledo Christian School, or TCS, the private Christian academy I attended from kindergarten through grade twelve. Our mascot was the eagle, and bold letters across the gymnasium wall reminded every student of the promise in Isaiah 40:31.

> Those who hope in the LORD will renew their strength. They
> will soar on wings like eagles; they will run and not grow weary,
> they will walk and not be faint. (NIV)

"Those who hope" meant that with God's help even the Barf King could soar. I believed those words back then. And despite the staggering number of students I meet who seem proudly jaded by their Christian school experience, I still believe those words today.

My mother worked as the school secretary, which meant I was the first kid through the doors every morning and the last to leave every afternoon. I would sit there in my pleated corduroys and mushroom-shaped eighties haircut, staring out her office window as the other kids streamed from class, textbooks stuffed into backpacks. Laughter echoed as they headed off to ride bikes and play *Super Mario Bros.* The glorious sounds of freedom. While I was still in school.

"Matthew, could you grab the new announcement sheet from Mrs. Rumschlag?" Mom would call over. "And run off a hundred or so copies for me after that?"

"Sure, Mom," I would reply.

Remembering childhood is like looking back through old yearbooks. Snapshots and random memories, some blurry and others crystal clear. Old friends and enemies. Highlights and lows. Psychologists say those early moments shape the rest of our lives.

I remember sitting on the floor in front of my first-grade teacher, Mrs. LaPrarie, repeating after her with my classmates, *"Obedience is doing what you're told, when you're told to do it, with a smile on your face."* I wanted nothing more than to live up to those words. Maybe that's why I still feel a little heartbroken when I think about the first time I was sent to the principal's office. I was caught in the middle of a misunderstanding and paddled for something I didn't do.

I would've preferred that paddle in the hands of a coldhearted villain. I could've been bitter about it, had someone bad to blame. But Mr. Gagle? Glasses and a mustache, friendly, funny, kindhearted to all. He was short but walked with a sense of towering joy. I loved him. Most everybody did.

The shame was overwhelming to me, being the "bad kid" sitting across from such a good man. Graciously, he called Mom down from her office to take the swing, which wound up being more of a bunt. Maybe that was Mr. G.'s way of saying, "I know you're a good kid, Matt, but I gotta do it." Or maybe that's just what I wanted him to think.

My third-grade teacher was feared for her cruel, superstrict demeanor. There's a quote that goes, "Be kind, for everyone you meet is fighting a hard battle." Maybe Mrs. Duval's battle was hard. Tough to see it that way when you feel like your teacher hates you.

The stress became worse, and Mom finally took me to the doctor for tests. I can still feel the cold exam table under my hospital gown as they handed me a chalky substance to drink. They pumped the rest up into my gut so they could get all their X-rays. I tried to lie still and not cry as a nurse shoved a long tube the wrong way up a one-way street.

"Good job, Matt!" the nurse said when it was over, like I was a puppy they were trying to housebreak. A mammoth toilet, twice as deep as the standard bowl, mocked me as I ran into the bathroom.

Official diagnosis: irritable bowel syndrome. IBS at age eight. Thanks, third grade.

School days at TCS have overshadowed many of my childhood memories, but I can still picture the nights and weekends that our family spent at church. It was rare for the Hammitts to miss Sunday morning worship, Wednesday night classes, or potlucks in the fellowship hall. Mom volunteered while my father, who worked as a software engineer, served on the board.

I didn't know it at the time, but some members of the church board had privately expressed concerns to our pastor. Those concerns were taken to heart, but not in the way they had hoped. One Sunday, in front of the whole church, those board members—including my dad—were told to leave. As in "leave and don't come back."

Church life, social life, everything stopped. These people were our family, all smiles, all love. Then suddenly they're avoiding us in the grocery store. I was eight years old. Too young to understand. But you never forget the way it feels to be cast out.

Mom and Dad acted like they were fine, but I think they were trying to shield me and my brother, or maybe even themselves. We found a new church home where we were welcomed with open arms. Dad started serving again, teaching Sunday school, getting involved in various aspects of outreach and ministry. Our new pastor was a gifted teacher and kind man, genuinely loved by his congregation. In a way, it seemed he was righting the wrongs of our previous pastor. I wish it could have been so simple.

There was more to it, of course, but from my point of view, our new pastor just disappeared one day. Must've been hard for Mom and Dad to tell me the truth, that our pastor was having an affair. With another man.

A new preacher came into the fold. Before long, the church split yet again. I wasn't sure how to process that pain, but I felt back then what I know for certain now. People are people. I never blamed God for those wounds, but I carried them. Maybe I still do.

My parents remained through multiple pastors, changes, and splits. They were a picture of grace and faithfulness in a world that's fractured and fickle. I'm so grateful for the way they have selflessly loved God, the church, each other, and me.

———

Things took a turn for the better in fourth grade when I entered Mrs. Segler's world. Every year Mrs. Segler directed a class play, and that year she cast me—yes, *anxious me*—in the starring role. The play was called *Tales of the Kingdom,* and I played Scarboy, an orphan ridiculed for the unsightly scar on his face. As the story evolves, Scarboy finds his place in the world through the power of love and is given a new name, Hero. This was far more than a tale to me. It was a life-changing lesson of how grace teaches us to wear our scars with dignity. I didn't just play the part of Scarboy—I *was* Scarboy. And being up there performing? It felt like maybe I had found my place in the world too.

Mrs. Segler's confidence changed everything. I've heard it said that we should do for one person what we wish we could do for many.

I'm so grateful that Mrs. Segler chose *anxious me* to be her Hero that year.

––––––––––

The tongue has the power of life and death, and those who love it will eat its fruit. (Proverbs 18:21, NIV)

Throughout the Bible, names carry the weight of hopes and dreams, calling, vocation, and sometimes prophetic vision. When someone is given a name, it can come with a blessing or a curse.

Funny how I took a ridiculous name like Barf King to heart when I was a kid. Perhaps the pain of taking that name has kept me from embracing the names and titles that describe my work.

"So, what do you do?"

The person asking may not see it through my smile or hear it in my voice, but that simple, cordial question from a stranger sets me on edge. It's not that I don't have anything to say, and I certainly don't have anything to be ashamed of. It's just that I do a lot of different things, and it's difficult to explain. Artist, singer, songwriter, author, speaker, and so on.

I catch myself dancing around those words. Claiming these titles, even though they describe what I do for a living, makes me feel pretentious. Regardless of the success I've experienced along the way, I still feel like a wannabe, a poser, a dreamer, clumsily trying to validate myself to strangers.

That's cute, they'll think. *Still chasing dreams at forty . . .*

Sometimes I'll just reply that I'm a musician. "You should try out for American Idol!" They offer this great piece of advice with a proud look, as if no one has ever suggested that to me before.

"Maybe I will!" I reply with a smile, because it's not worth explaining that I'm already published or how the world won't benefit from another idol these days.

Instead of embracing the titles that come with my calling or receiving the blessing of the name my parents gave me, Matthew, which means "gift from God," I've carried the curses of others close to my heart. I keep fighting the feeling that I'm a child in a grown-up's world.

The War Within

True courage is being afraid, and going ahead
and doing your job anyhow.

—GENERAL H. NORMAN SCHWARZKOPF JR.

Only at a small Christian school would the principal also teach fifth grade. But hey, I was more than happy to get Mr. G.

The Gulf War was raging, Saddam Hussein was America's arch-nemesis #1 and Mr. G. was a member of the army reserves. I had just added a General Schwarzkopf to my Desert Storm trading-card collection, so I was psyched when we started talking about the war at school. One day Mr. G. brought his army-issued hazmat suit in for us to pass around. The suit came to my desk. I figured it would be camouflage, but the pants were the exact same color as the dark khakis I had on.

I slipped the hazmat pants over my khakis, slid my arms through the jacket and pulled the gas mask down over my head. The army suit made me feel bold and mighty, ready for some secret mission, like Rambo or G. I. Joe. "Hurry up, Matt," River Wilson said. "It's my turn."

I took off the jacket and quickly yanked the hazmat pants down. The whole class broke out in hysterics.

Did Mr. G. say something funny? Why is everybody laughing?

I looked down. Not one, but two pairs of pants around my ankles.

So there I stood for what seemed like twelve solid minutes in my Hanes-brand tighty-whities. Have you ever had that dream where you're caught at school in your underwear? This was not a dream.

Mr. G. slid his arm around me and guided me to the hall. I tried really hard to hold back tears. "It's okay, Matt," Mr. G. said. "Everybody makes mistakes. Someday you'll look back on this and laugh too."

Mr. G. was nice but such scenarios are bully bait. Bullies seize upon the weaknesses of others, out of fear that someone will expose theirs first. Reality is harsh, even in a Christian school. Sometimes, especially at a Christian school.

Brad Lane gave me fifth-grade hell after that incident with the pants. Brad had a withered arm, limp from birth. Maybe that's why he felt the need to strong-arm us smaller kids with the other one. Headlocks, noogies, pulling my chair out from under me while I was eating lunch.

One day Brad smacked me in the head while passing in a crowded hall. I tripped and my books scattered. I'd finally had enough. "You wanna go?" I demanded, throwing my fists up. I'd heard that in a movie, I think. I paired it with the most menacing face I could possibly make.

"Go where, stupid?" Brad shot back. Fair question, I suppose.

The kids all laughed like I was Charlie Brown whiffing the football again. I picked up my books, hung my head, and walked away.

———

I've thought long and hard about what made me such an anxious child. I was part of a loving family, and I even asked my mother about it while writing this book. She said I seemed happy on the outside. Besides the struggles with anxiety and school-bully stuff, I have a lot of wonderful memories from childhood.

I used to get hung up on finding reasons for everything, but these days I've learned to rest in the mystery. Much like the apostle Paul, we all have our thorns. I guess God made me really sensitive. That's my thorn. Or at least one of them. Isaiah 40:31 says God gives power to the faint and strength to those with no might. I just needed to trust that He would turn those thorny parts of my life into something good.

My Cardboard Rocket Ship

If you cannot teach me to fly, teach me to sing.

—Sir James Barrie, Peter Pan

My parents loved music, so we always had a lot of records around the house, mostly Christian and gospel. Growing up, I listened to *Kids Praise!* with Psalty the Singing Songbook and learned about the fruit of the Spirit from The Music Machine. Later, I became familiar with artists such as Amy Grant, the Imperials, and Michael W. Smith.

Every now and then my folks would pull out their collection of old vinyl, and we'd listen to The Beatles, Joni Mitchell, and my favorite, The Monkees.

My folks weren't musical in the performing sense, but every once in a while, my dad would play his accordion for laughs. At least I think it was for laughs. He might've been trying to show off his chops. (No offense, Dad, but I didn't catch the polka bug.)

Inspiration came from outside my home as well. My Aunt Etta was in her early twenties and still lived with my grandparents. Aunt Etta was cool, soft spoken, and deep with her wide-rimmed glasses and long brown hair. I spent a lot of time with her back then, and her radio was dialed 24-7 to 92.5 KISS FM. I'll never forget the first time I heard "In the Air Tonight" by Phil Collins or The Police's "Every Breath You Take." Those classic melodies became a huge part of my musical DNA, but it wasn't until high school that my brother, Aaron, showed me how to express it for myself.

I never felt cooler than when Aaron invited me into his room to listen to those classic Petra albums. I'd be like, "Aaron, can you show me how to play that chord?"

Aaron would position my fingers on the strings of his red guitar until what I was playing sounded like the song, and it felt like I was part of the band.

After that, I would sneak off every chance I had to pick up the guitar, sit behind a drum kit, or get my hands on a piano. Sometimes I'd play other people's songs, but mostly I would create a bed of chords that matched the way I was feeling inside. Words and melodies flowed naturally over the chords. Sometimes they made sense, other times they didn't. Still, it was my life, my heart, my own way of worship.

I wrote my first real song when I was sixteen and called it "Coffee of Life."

Jump into my cardboard rocket ship
I'm going somewhere you'll never forget
into my magic time machine
I'll take you somewhere
you held no regrets

When I was a boy, my dad bought us this giant multicolored cardboard rocket ship. I loved climbing into that thing and escaping the harsh gravity of this world for a while, lost in wonder, finding a place where I better belonged. In a sense, music was like that rocket ship. With songwriting, it was as if I could create something from nothing, pulling meaning and beauty from thin air. I thought maybe, in some small way, that's what God felt like when He created the stars and planets, when He created me.

In the image of my Father, I wanted to be a creator too.

———————

So God created mankind in his own image, in the image of God he created them; male and female he created them. (Genesis 1:27, NIV)

In the beginning, God created the heavens and the earth, and it was a good and perfect world. He created contrast and color, a dance between earth and sky by hanging great lights in the heavens. He filled the oceans and the earth with diverse and gracefully complex life. He gave Adam a beautiful woman to share it with, and all that was beautiful thrived.

Don't we all wish it was still a perfect world?

Sang-tus Reel

Chris Rohman was a tall, skinny kid with wavy black hair, the kind of hair that God bestows on natural-born rock stars. I was not a natural-born rocker. Maybe that's one of the reasons I was drawn to Chris.

One day I saw Chris perched on a table in the lunchroom, playing Tom Petty's "Wildflowers" on his guitar. I walked over, and he told me that he'd learned the song to impress a girl. *Wow, okay,* I thought. *Music is this guy's language, just like me.*

Some older students took note and invited us to join Toledo Christian's chapel band. That's where we started to lock in musically. Practice once a week didn't cut it, so we met on weekends to jam in Chris's basement on our favorites by bands like Weezer, the Foo Fighters, and Jimmy Eat World. Chris was the better guitarist, so I played drums, and our buddy Matt Kollar joined in on bass.

Chris's mom fed us an endless supply of Twinkies and Cheez Whiz, and his dad, Jim, inspired us to play classic rockers like "Funk #49" by Joe Walsh's James Gang and "White Room" by Cream. Before long, our influences merged with our faith and creativity, and the songs of our youth began to take shape.

We auditioned a few lead singers, but none of them worked out in the long run. Chris finally spoke up. "Matt, you can sort of sing—right?"

"I guess," I shrugged. "I'll at least give it a try."

We found our groove, literally, when drummer Mark Graalman came on board. (Okay, I confess: we stole him from another band. Sorry, other band.) Mark was eighteen, had just graduated from high school, and had a heart as big as his drumbeat. He soon became the glue that held our new band together, both onstage and off.

Over the course of my career with Sanctus Real, I've been asked a lot about how the band got started. But there's one question I've been asked more than any other, one that I've had to explain to every single fan, friend, and interviewer, every single time. "How did you get your name?"

Here's the scoop. One day Mark told us he'd found a word in the dictionary that meant "holy; set apart; a hymn of praise." All things that we desired our band and music to be. The word was *Sanctus*.

We tagged it with *Real* to represent our desire to be authentic both personally and musically. The final vote took place, and "Sanctus Real" it was.

Truth is, we had no idea how to pronounce the Latin word *Sanctus* back then. So our band name turned out to be a Latin word with English pronunciation coupled with an English word that could also be Latin. Understand? No? It's okay. Everyone knows band names don't have to make sense, as long as you know how to say them. So, if you say "Sang-tus Reel," you'll be in real good shape.

———

Our first show was in November of 1996 in Jim Rohman's photography studio. With his long hair and quirky-cool personality, Jim was more rock 'n' roll than all of us put together.

Jim's studio was in a row of brick warehouses where we could make all the noise we wanted after Sensei Jay's karate class let out next door. We set up a stage and practiced our handful of original songs until we could play them backward in our sleep. After dialing in our Peavey sound system and mounting a few can lights, we slid the studio's garage door open and let a crowd of fifty or so friends and family in, enticing them with free food before the show.

The first Sanctus Real show still survives on VHS somewhere. It's a little grainy, and man, was I nervous. But you can see it in my eyes at that very first gig: I was also hooked.

Sanctus Real ushered in a golden era of *new*. Even difficult experiences seemed exhilarating. I have no doubt that I sounded awful the first time I plugged in an electric guitar or sang through a live microphone, but people actually *liked* the first song I wrote. My first time onstage, and the crowd *applauded*. I got an MTV haircut, and people said it was *cool*. Kids who used to make fun of me said that I was *good*.

First guitar. First amp. First pair of Chuck Taylors. First cool stage clothes. First van ride to a gig with my new band. For the first time in my life, *new* was something good. I felt a long way from the Barf King.

5

Road Less Traveled

> I took the one less traveled by, and that has
> made all the difference.
>
> —ROBERT FROST

My last two years of high school were consumed with church and music. We played anywhere and everywhere we could. Bowling alleys, youth rallies, lock-ins, pizza parties, all-ages bars, and bar mitzvahs. It's all kind of fuzzy, so I might be remembering that last one wrong.

At the same time, I led worship for my church youth group and provided special music for meetings and retreats. My one passion was to express life and faith through music, but that didn't always leave a lot of time for stuff like school or dating and friends.

I graduated with the class of '98 and traded college to pursue a music career. My parents had always been supportive, but my youth pastor had helped by clearing the way for me years before.

"I think God might be calling Matt to more of a nontraditional path," Pastor Bill told them. "Pray about it. Encourage him the best that you can." Call it prophetic or just a hunch, but those words helped my parents make peace with me skipping college and climbing into a van with my guitar.

Shortly after, Sanctus Real released our first full-length album called *Message for the Masses*. It was DIY guitar-rock, recorded in a garage, and totally funded by the band. I worked odd jobs to help pitch in. Retail. Day care. The worst was telemarketing.

Telemarketing paid well, but it was relentless in the age before universal cell phones and caller ID. I always felt we were targeting people at the most inconvenient times in hopes that they'd agree to buy something just to get us off the phone.

We were hawking auto glass, and I had to follow a written script. Keeping people on the line required a certain mix of trickery and assertiveness, neither of which I am gifted with. Most people didn't listen long. Profanities rained down upon us. Death threats were not uncommon. One guy with a deep, gravelly voice told me he knew where I lived and swore to put my head through his windshield and make me his hood ornament. I knew this was theoretically impossible, but the conviction of his tone still made me sweat.

As an aspiring Christian singer, I couldn't help but think about the scripts church people sometimes use to evangelize. How they meant well—but often, in the effort to "win just one," ended up driving away multitudes instead. The job was truly dreadful, but it taught me a key lesson. I didn't want to be some telemarketer for Jesus. I wanted to offer something deeper than gospel sales pitches and religious clichés. To listen and not just talk. To meet God and people in a place that was real.

It was a humble beginning, but still I was living out my fantasy. Playing shows with my buddies, writing songs, releasing CDs. Telling people about God's goodness and how He was working in my life.

But late at night, a God-given desire stirred in my heart. Some important part of the puzzle that remained incomplete. At the end of the day, I knew living the dream would not validate my every longing.

So I prayed and asked God to show me what He wanted for my life. I did my best to trust and let go.

And then, I met a girl.

6

Sarah

You have stolen my heart with one glance
of your eyes.

—Song of Songs 4:9, NIV

I was standing under the big white merchandise tent at the Uthtopia Music Festival in Columbus, Ohio. The sun had set, but the stage lights were illuminating the area where she was standing, across the field from me. Long blond hair, denim overalls. Barefoot, laughing, dancing, hands in the air. You could tell she did not care about what anyone thought. This girl was free.

I drifted to the edge of the tent for a better look. She swayed with arms lifted as music split the cool air. In that moment my whole world was in slow motion, as if the crowd and the music had all faded, except for this one girl. More than anything, it was her smile that had me both lost and found. Innocence. Joy. Confidence.

Whatever she had, I needed more of it in my life. *I have to meet this girl.*

But I couldn't be that bold. I was nineteen and had kissed dating goodbye. *Just me and Jesus for a year,* I reminded myself. *God will bring me the right person in the right time.*

But what if this *was* the right time? Doesn't faith require action? What is the balance between God's plan and my choices? Back and forth, I was pulled and pushed like a magnet that kept flipping sides. Make a move? *Let her be.* Make it happen? *Trust God, wait and pray.*

A kid tapped my shoulder. "Hey, aren't you the singer for that band that played earlier today?"

"Oh, uh, yeah," I replied. "Thanks for watching us." Some others walked over to talk with me about the band. I tried my best to be polite, impatient to break away. By the time I made it back to the edge of the tent, the girl in the overalls had disappeared.

My heart sank. I'd waited too long. *Oh well. Guess it wasn't meant to be.*

———

We made the three-hour drive from Columbus back home to Toledo, where we were set to perform at a community-wide worship event the next morning. The band huddled in a circle and prayed like we always did before shows, arms around shoulders, anticipating great things.

A few hundred people were scattered across the lawn at Woodlands Park in the sparkling suburb of Perrysburg. I strapped on my sea-green Strat, and Mark counted us in as I stepped toward the microphone.

I looked out over the crowd and spotted a few familiar faces. My eyes wandered farther back, scanning the audience to the right, then left. Suddenly, there she was. The overalls girl. Not in overalls this time. Wearing cute glasses and a sundress. But still. Carefree, confident smile. Sparkling eyes.

NO WAY.

I'd be lying if I said I wasn't distracted from worship that morning, but believe me, I was giving thanks to God for offering me a second chance. And even though my heart was pounding double time, I wasn't going to miss the opportunity again. After we wrapped up our set, I dropped my guitar and headed over to introduce myself. Onstage I could hide behind a microphone and guitar, pretending I was collected and cool. But offstage, the voice in my head reminded me I was still the Barf King. *Be smooth,* I told myself. *But not too smooth.*

"Um, hey! Hi," I began. "I think I saw you at the festival yesterday? I'm Matt."

"Oh yeah. Hey," she said, shaking my hand. "Sarah."

Sarah's whole family was with her. Mom, dad, grandma. Little sister. I shook all their hands too. "Sarah's glasses are fake," her little sister reported.

"Oh," I replied. "Ha, okay . . ."

Sarah swept her sister to the side, and we exchanged the basics. She was home from college and would be headed down to Ohio State after the break. Major undecided. In the meantime she was staying with her parents in Perrysburg. She briefly mentioned some other guy but didn't define him as a boyfriend or anything. Was she dropping a hint? And was the hint *No, there's someone else* or *Yes, I'm available*?

Torn again. Do I try and risk failure? Fail because I didn't even try? Did I mention I did not have a lot of experience with dating? I had a couple of girlfriends in high school, but I was never the kind of guy to date around. Even the thought of inviting a girl I didn't know to hang out was nerve racking. But a lack of courage is different from stupidity, and I knew Sarah was something special.

Sometimes God opens a door. Other times, a window. My window was closing fast. The small talk was over, and it was time to go our separate ways. I gathered up every bit of courage I had. "Hey, you, uh"—I paused, lost in her sparkling blue eyes—"think maybe I could get your number so we could hang out sometime?"

"Okay," she said. "Sure."

I wrote down her digits with a fine-point Sharpie on a yellow sticky note and floated back to the stage. I have never enjoyed wrapping guitar cables as much in my life as I did that day. All I could think about was her. Every few minutes I would take out that sticky note and stare at her name and number, certain that all things were working together for the good.

Hey, guys, this is Sarah. I love hearing Matt's version of our story, but mine actually began nine months earlier. It was my freshman year of college, and to be honest, I was a party girl. Nothing criminal or promiscuous, just drinking with friends sometimes. Okay, like almost every night. Anyway, over Christmas break, I went to an event where Matt was leading worship. I saw him onstage and immediately felt that spark, the "connection." *Okay, God,* I prayed, *I'll quit drinking if you let me marry that guy.*

Three days after asking Sarah if she wanted to hang out, I walked up to her parents' front door with a plate of chocolate-cherry brownies that I'd baked for her, still hot, covered with foil. I could feel the weight in that one sweet moment, the anticipation, the anxiety and hope. I could feel all that stuff about purpose and plans and life swirling around me, like a crossroads, I guess.

Dirty-faced kids rode bikes in the street, and dogs barked in the distance. A tiny white jet streamed slowly across the sky. I took a deep breath and knocked.

The door opened. Sarah invited me in. I followed her back to the kitchen. A pair of work jeans and dirty white sneakers stuck out from under the sink. "Hey, Matt," Sarah's dad, Bill, called. "Dishwasher's acting up."

"Sorry to hear," I replied, wanting to help but not knowing a thing about appliances. I took a look around. Their house wasn't a mess, but they sure hadn't gone to any trouble to straighten up. Sarah had on a baggy sweatshirt, holes in her pants. *Pretty cool,* I thought. Nobody was trying to impress me. The attitude was come on in, just as you are.

"Bill, she's still breathing!" a distraught voice yelled from the backyard. It was Sarah's mom.

"C'mon, Pam, she's been dead for two days!" Bill shouted back.

"You mind comin' outside a sec?" Sarah asked me. "We have to bury our dog."

I followed Sarah and her dad out to the backyard where her brother, sister, and mom were already gathered around a shallow grave. At the bottom, a carefully wrapped plastic bag held their beloved dog, Hattie. Pam had cut a small breathing hole by Hattie's mouth "just in case." They offered a prayer of thanks for the old girl and said their final goodbyes.

Sarah and I walked back into the kitchen. "Oh. Here ya go," I told Sarah, handing her the plate of brownies that I'd forgotten about.

She peeled back the foil and took a tiny bite. "Sorry," she said. "I don't have much of a sweet tooth."

Maybe I should have been hurt, but you know how most people would have acted like those brownies were delicious and then later threw them in the trash? How you think you know somebody, but it turns out they're just putting on a front? I knew right then that wasn't Sarah. Sarah did not pretend. And I loved that.

We sat on the back porch, just the two of us, and talked into the early hours of the morning.

I had just come home from a missions trip with Campus Crusade for Christ, where I'd rededicated my life. There was this other guy on the trip. Sort of. But after that first night with Matt, it was over. I was 100 percent all in. —Sarah

7

Grass Roots

S anctus Real didn't have songs on the radio yet, and YouTube was a dream waiting to be born above a pizzeria and a Japanese restaurant in San Mateo, California. MySpace was barely off the ground and the best way to spread the news about your music was still word of mouth. Problem was, word of mouth was really SLOW back then. Like literally, someone came to our show and then told a friend we were good and maybe played the friend a song from our CD. Hopefully that friend would tell another friend. Grass roots was the only way to go viral in 1999, and you had to play as many live shows as possible to keep people talking about your band.

Fortunately for us, there was a huge youth movement in churches throughout the late nineties. More youth meant more opportunities for four fresh-faced, (semi) clean-cut young men playing upbeat rock songs with a Christian message. Adults were eager to fund these efforts, and everybody seemed to have a budget to hire a band for their next big youth event.

Sanctus Real stayed busy, taking pretty much any show that came our way. We became well acquainted with the love offering system, sometimes even showing up and hoping for the best. Looking back, those were good times: playing for the youth in some backwoods town between Bowling Green, Ohio, and Battle Creek, Michigan. The audience might have been small, but when the kids got fired up, there was no feeling like it.

It wasn't uncommon for the pastor to grab the mic at the end of the night and say something like, "Church, let's bless these young men and put a little gas in their van," while winking at us and nodding to the ushers, who would start passing empty KFC buckets down each pew.

After the show, there'd be a stack of pizzas waiting in the fellowship hall and some nice church lady would have made a cake with the band's name piped on top. Pretty cool when an eighty-year-old woman manages to spell *Sanctus Real* right. We'd say goodbye in the parking lot after a whole bunch of hugs and prayers for safe travel. Just before we'd drive away, the preacher would slide an envelope into my hand.

"Bless y'all," he'd say. "Come back anytime you can."

"Yes, sir," I would reply. "Thanks."

I've never been a gambler, but opening those envelopes felt like scratching off a lotto ticket. I'd get that nervous feeling, knowing it could be a note saying, "Thank you, come again!" or coupons for ice cream sundaes from McDonald's. You just never knew.

Thankfully, more often than not, we'd get a stack of small bills with a Benjamin or two on the bottom from a parent who believed in our mission or simply stood by the principle that a worker was worth his wage. Regardless of how much cash we took home, we remained thankful for the opportunity to play music—and always grateful when our van and trailer made it to the next town.

8

Sparks

Sarah wasn't the least bit impressed that I was the lead singer of a rock band. She was supportive, interested in my hopes and dreams. But she could not have cared less about status or image. Above all, she focused on what she believed was right and didn't shy away from expressing it.

I never considered myself to be image conscious, but compared with Sarah I was a lot more worried about people's opinions than I had realized. She challenged me to be better. Which sort of bugged me but also made me love her that much more.

I learned quickly that Sarah's way of investing in a relationship was far different from mine. I went overboard to keep the peace. She would dive in like a kamikaze, continuing to speak her mind even if she knew it might rock the boat or sink the entire ship. Bold, blunt, no filter. Completely the opposite of people-pleaser me. I tried to keep my appearance so filtered and polished, always anxious about saying the right things at the right times. It was as if Sarah was beyond all that.

Matt and I both wanted peace; we just went about it in different ways. I was born bold and blunt, which has been both a blessing and a curse through the years. —Sarah

Sarah and I took our relationship seriously, so we set out to take things slow, mostly hanging out, walking the neighborhood, splitting a chocolate-chip cookie and cream-cheese sandwich at Beekman's Bagels, romping like school kids on the playgrounds around Perrysburg.

Sanctus Real was still a regional act, so the sting of long distance wasn't as painful as I feared it would be. She was still taking classes in Columbus, and I was out playing shows most weekends, but we managed to see each other on a regular basis. When she wasn't able to make it to Perrysburg, I would happily make the three-hour drive to Ohio State, even if it was just to catch a few hours together.

In the late nineties a lot of couples couldn't survive being miles apart. Cellular plans, especially long-distance calls, were expensive, so neither of us kept a cell phone. There was email, but it took about five minutes to dial in and the computer made a sound like it was strangling a duck. I realize this sounds like ancient history, but it was barely twenty years ago.

As the relationship grew deeper, Sarah and I spent a lot of time together on the beat-up red couch on her parents' back sunporch, talking about life and plans or sometimes just sitting in silence, content to be close to each other.

The True Love Waits movement was big in those days. Purity rings and chastity rallies were standard in evangelical communities. Those movements take a lot of flak these days, but restricting the physical really does force you to talk. It's a lot easier to make out than make conversation, but do you truly get to know each other that way?

I remember one night we were on that red-striped couch, sitting at opposite ends as usual. But somehow on this night our feet touched just the slightest bit. I could feel the electricity as we pushed the bare skin of our feet closer together. That burning feeling slowly rose up through my body, and I could barely breathe.

It would still be over a month before we shared a simple kiss, but if there was any doubt that Sarah and I were more than just friends, it was settled for me that night.

Oh, gosh, me too. The chemistry. That "feeling." It was almost unbearable. —Sarah

As we were getting to know each other, those few simple touches felt so significant. There's a debate in the world as to whether there's one perfect mate out there for each person. To me, it didn't matter. I had no doubt that I'd found "the one" for me.

So I bought a ring.

9

A Breakthrough

Commit to the LORD whatever you do,

and he will establish your plans.

—PROVERBS 16:3, NIV.

The band kept hammering away, playing more shows, trying to get the word out. A lot of prospects teased, but we were still considered an indie band.

I'd bought a ring, and Sarah had decided to come home from Columbus so we could be together. Chris was taking college classes. It was make-it-or-break-it time. Did the band really want to keep going? We were always praying for a sign or some kind of breakthrough.

One day Mark told us about a contest that the local rock station, WIOT, was running to find the best local band.

At first, we were reluctant, concerned that a Christian band wouldn't be accepted by "Toledo's Home of the Rock." WIOT's playlist was a mix of classic rock bands such as Led Zeppelin and Aerosmith, along with new rockers like 3 Doors Down and Linkin Park.

We went back and forth as to whether we should enter, and at some point, Mark offered, "Why not? We've got nothing to lose."

Earlier that year, we'd saved up some cash to record three songs in Memphis with a producer named Skidd Mills. Skidd had worked with some of our favorite Christian bands, as well as with some artists who were already getting airplay on stations like WIOT. We knew that we'd need something more polished if we were ever going to be noticed.

Just before the deadline, Mark took a disc of "Won't Walk Away" down to WIOT and entered Sanctus Real in the contest. Seventy-five other local acts signed up, and a lot of them were really good. Many of these bands were older and more experienced. Some had opened for groups like Van Halen and The White Stripes. How could a Christian band from TCS hold up in a big rock radio contest? It was like David squaring off against the giant.

WIOT had a panel of industry judges. We survived each round until only ten of us remained. Then five. Then three.

In the summer of 2000, between cuts by Green Day and the Foo Fighters, Sanctus Real was voted northwest Ohio's best band.

Capturing the title kicked us up a notch. We were invited to do our first club show shortly thereafter and began to play venues outside the typical church and youth group circuit. I thought it was pretty cool that God would work that way, that after four years of hammering away, our big break comes through the local rock station. It didn't matter to us how the doors opened; we were grateful that God was moving in our midst.

Winning the contest gave us the confidence we needed to head back to Memphis and finish a full-length record with Skidd. That simple statement Mark made before he drove our song down to the radio station stuck with us. It would define a new season and a new attitude, and become the title of our new record. Truly, we had nothing to lose.

10

The Engagement

Now that I had a ring, I started brainstorming ideas for my proposal. I wanted it to be a surprise but special, something Sarah would never forget. I considered popping the question onstage during a show, singing her a song—but nah, that would be all about me.

I thought about her parents' sunporch where we'd forged the foundation of our relationship, talking, sharing dreams, acting silly, our feet occasionally brushing, electricity in the air. I could hide the ring in the couch cushions, drop some popcorn. Fish it out. I was planning to ask her early summer though, and there were a lot of spiders out there. I hate spiders, so maybe not.

Then, the perfect idea hit me. I would ask Sarah to marry me in a swimming pool. (Ask in the pool, not get married in the pool.) That would be romantic, right?

Actually, it was her grandmother's pool. Gloria was the matriarch of the family, and her swimming pool was the gathering place for everybody Sarah loved. Gloria lived in a humble little red house a few blocks down from Sarah's folks. Her pool was nothing fancy. In fact, her place was so unfancy that everybody went to the bathroom in Gloria's garage.

The door to the garage was close to the pool, and let's just say you wouldn't want to walk on the ancient shag carpet in the house with wet feet anyway. You might be getting the idea that there was a second bathroom in the garage. Nope, just the open end of a rusty drain pipe in the middle of a concrete floor, right out in the open, near a window with no shades. No door. No seat.

We just called it what is was—the pee hole. —Sarah

I know I can be overly concerned with people's opinions. But knowing something and changing it are two different things. Now I'm in a relationship with this girl who is so opposite and free. She has this rowdy, cut-loose, loving family, and I desperately want to fit in. We gather at her grandmother's pool, and it is totally relaxed and unpretentious. I want this in my life. I *need* it.

"By the way, where is the bathroom?"

"Oh, everybody goes in the garage, honey," Gloria said breezily, flashing her pearly white dentures with an uproarious laugh. "Just look for the hole, honey. Just look for the hole."

Change takes a leap of faith, and I admit, for a while I held it. Eventually, the desire to loosen up overruled my hang-ups, and soon enough I was standing at the sewer drain too.

I remember one day we were all gathered around the pool, hanging out and having fun when I dashed into the garage to visit the old pee hole. I could hear the muted laughter of these people I had grown to love outside. In that one moment, standing in the stale heat, peeing into a rusty sewer pipe, I felt completely at peace. I felt like I was exactly where I belonged.

Sarah and her grandmother were a lot alike, and looking into the future, I could see her gathered around her own pool with family and friends and kids scattered and laughing everywhere—and I wanted to be right there with her. It was a picture of the life I wanted for us.

So that settled it in my mind. This is where our life together would begin.

––––––––

On the big day, I safety-pinned the ring to the lining of my swim trunks. Double extra good because you don't want the .63 carat diamond you saved nine months to buy to get lost on the bottom of a pool.

It was that early evening time when things get quiet and still. The sun was sinking through the big maples in Gloria's backyard. Sarah and I were in the pool, no one else around.

I started to feel anxious but not in a bad way, just that way when you know something is about to take place that will change your entire life. I was about to become engaged to be married. (If she said yes, that is.)

After a quick trip to the garage to make sure the ring was secure, I dove back into the deep end, fumbling to unpin the ring. Vision blurred, eyes burning from chlorine, I swam up toward the most beautiful silhouette in the world.

"What's wrong?" Sarah asked as I came up for air.

"I'm nervous."

She moved closer as I lifted my hand from beneath the water, ring held tightly between my first finger and thumb. Sarah stared at the diamond as it sparkled in the setting sun. For a moment, she was confused. Confusion turned to surprise. Then she started to cry.

"I, um . . ." I had all these poetic things planned to say but couldn't get any of the words to come out right. "We've been seeing each other a long time now and, uh . . . Sarah?" Eyes red. Snot running out of my nose. "And. I just, uh, wanted to . . ."

Yes! Ha! I said YES! It was perfect! —Sarah

If we were to re-create the scene for television, it would show me sweeping Sarah up in that joyful moment, soft-lit by the setting sun, followed by a long, romantic kiss, eyes locked and filled with hope and wonder at the future that lies ahead. This is not what happened that day.

I picked him up. —Sarah

Bouncing and squawking happy noises into the evening air, Sarah lifted me up like a fish out of water. Maybe it wasn't the smoothest of engagements. Or the most glamorous. But Sarah said *yes*. She gave me the honor of putting a ring on her finger and agreed to take my name.

Things with Sanctus Real were taking off, and Sarah had school business to wrap up, so we set a date for the following summer. We had thirteen months before the wedding, and every minute felt like forever until she was mine.

The band was performing on weekends, but now that I was getting married, I needed to find a steady income and start saving up money while I still lived at home. I took a position at my church day care as one of the teachers for the four- and five-year-olds. Here's a snapshot of my typical day.

"Mr. Matt, Mr. Matt!"

"It's nap time, shhh!" I whispered loudly.

"Mr. Matt, look what I did!" said Martha, a proud smile stretched across her tiny face. Martha had snuck a pen in her pocket for nap time.

She didn't have any paper, so she covered her hands, face, arms, and legs—head to toe—in doodles. And her mom was picking her up in twenty minutes.

Looking back, I'm not sure which job was more rock 'n' roll, Sanctus Real or day care.

While I was herding preschoolers, Sarah was learning to cut hair at cosmetology school on the east side of Toledo. Success in the music business is like the wind, but hair? Well, one of us needed job security.

In the evenings we would cuddle up and talk, dreaming of a day when one of us wouldn't have to leave and say goodnight.

11

Nothing to Lose

The Skidd Mills–produced *Nothing to Lose* came out in 2001 on our very own SpinsAround Records. The sound was heartland garage rock with crunchy guitars and catchy melodies, polished but still raw. Chris designed our album artwork, and his dad did the photos. We sold copies at live shows and promoted it wherever people would listen, praying that God would use *Nothing to Lose* to catapult Sanctus Real to that next level. Next level had a GPS coordinate in our world—36.1468° N, 86.7938° W. Christian Hollywood: Nashville, Tennessee.

Each year, the Gospel Music Association hosted GMA Week. Christian music industry insiders would gather in Nashville to network, promote artists, and most importantly for us, discover new talent. Record labels would plaster the halls, floors, and elevator doors of the Renaissance Hotel with the faces of famous or emerging Christian music stars. They would even cover the sky bridge from the hotel to the convention center. The festivities would end with the annual Dove Awards show, where the most successful artists would walk away with a handful of bronze trophies for their latest efforts.

We couldn't afford to send the whole band, so Chris and Mark stuffed their backpacks with *Nothing to Lose* CDs and followed that yellow brick road to Music City for GMA Week.

They stood on street corners and hung out in hotel lobbies, handing CDs to anybody who looked important or carried herself like she could help a young, struggling band catch a break.

It was a bit humbling to pawn our project on street corners, but you gotta put yourself out there. *Nothing to Lose,* right? By the end of GMA Week, we had planted hundreds of seeds in Nashville. Mark and Chris drove home, and we continued working to promote our album, trying not to obsess over getting a call from Tennessee.

Ecclesiastes says to sow your seeds and keep working, because you can never be sure which seeds will take. Be faithful, do your best, and leave the rest up to the One who gives the growth. In this case, it didn't take long before we started getting calls from record labels who wanted to explore whether they could help our band grow.

One of the first calls we received came from Tooth and Nail Records in Seattle. I tried to play down my excitement because Tooth and Nail bands were a huge part of the soundtrack to my teenage years. The calls kept coming, and eventually nearly every Christian label expressed interest in Sanctus Real.

A young A&R guy from Sparrow Records named Chris York flew out to see us perform in Toledo. He was kind, but everyone knew it wasn't our best performance. Instead of pulling out his pen and record contract ('cause that's how we thought it worked back then), he encouraged us to keep practicing. We continued to receive calls, even from mainstream companies who didn't focus on Christian music but liked the novelty of a rock band with lyrics about God.

Back then there was some debate as to whether there should be "Christian bands" or just bands with musicians who happened to be

Christians. You don't buy "Christian bread" at the store, even if it's made by a believer. You don't drive a "Christian car" because it's designed by a follower of Jesus. The argument went something along those lines.

I suppose having a genre of music called "Christian" was simply a way to let people know they were buying songs that would encourage their faith, and I think that's needed in the world. On the other hand, I understand that followers of Christ can make good art that speaks for itself.

I'll admit, though, at the time this debate caused us to do some soul searching as we made decisions about our future. Did we want to be the alternative rock band with a Christian message? Or the Christian band that played alternative rock?

Mainstream was called secular music by evangelicals back then. Secular means worldly, nonspiritual. Those who "went secular" sold out. I remember seeing DC Talk in concert as one of their songs was gaining traction on secular pop radio. With his right hand raised toward heaven, Toby reassured the crowd, "If DC Talk crosses over, we're taking the Cross over." Clearly, they had their finger on the pulse of the evangelical world, knowing that without reassurance their core audience might turn away.

There's not much debate over secular versus Christian these days, but it was something you had to consider back then. All in all, the future looked bright for Sanctus Real. The nineties were over. Y2K had come and gone, and the world hadn't crashed down in flames. Record labels were taking note as our momentum continued to grow. Best of all for me, it was finally summer.

12

Beautiful Day

For this reason a man shall leave his father and
his mother, and be joined to his wife; and they
shall become one flesh.

—GENESIS 2:24, NASB

My wedding was fast approaching. Sanctus Real wasn't a job where you could clock in at nine and out at five with an hour break for lunch. The work was all day, every day, and all-consuming, and it looked like things were finally starting to break. In the process, I didn't give much time to helping Sarah prepare.

But wasn't she supposed to plan the wedding? I mean, as a little girl, Sarah was dreaming about her fairy-tale wedding while I was blowing up G. I. Joes in my sandbox. She'd take care of the details, working on her dream while I was busy with mine. At least that's the way I thought it worked at the time.

She did assign me one job. Making the official wedding program. You know: My name, her name. Date/time/location. Flower girl. Ring bearer. Special music. Bible verse. Vows. Rings. Song while the bride and groom exit. Everybody leaves.

Simple enough. It's like making a set list, and I could do that in my sleep. It seemed so simple that a week before the ceremony, I still didn't have one made.

"Please tell me you have the program," Sarah said.

"Yeah, totally," I replied. "No problem." How hard could it be? I'm a creative type. Chic font, a few classy graphics. Type it up and run off a bunch of copies on fancy paper. I've been making copies since I was, like, age five.

"Please just do this *one* thing, Matt," she said, with a deep and prophetic sigh. "Don't put it off to the last minute. Please?"

"I got this, babe," I assured her, gently squeezing her hand. "You can count on me."

I put it off to the last minute. The wedding was on Saturday, and Friday night I was like, *Seems like there was something I was s'posed to do . . .*

Even though the program was a little hasty, at noon on July 14, 2001, we all dressed up, filed down the center aisle, and stood at the altar of Calvary Assembly of God.

I remember my bridesmaids dancing around me to the sound-track of *My Best Friend's Wedding* . . . the smell of Matt's bouton-niere . . . the scent of cologne on his tux . . . —Sarah

Sarah wore a strapless princess dress with peachy pink flowers. Lace and pearls, her hair in a Cinderella bun. I wore a black tuxedo with a silk mocha tie. Sarah looked like a vision of love and, well, some people say I looked like Ellen DeGeneres. Hey, I was a musician in 2001. What can I say?

Pastor Bill performed the ceremony. It's a blur now, but I vowed to love, honor, and cherish my bride for life. I bound myself to her through thick and thin and sickness and health and even when it was really, really hard and I wanted to quit.

Sarah agreed to the same. The young people looked hopeful, and the older ones looked pleased, yet pensive, like maybe we weren't completely sure about what we were getting ourselves into. But reality would hit soon enough, so hey, enjoy the honeymoon.

U2's "Beautiful Day" played in the background as we took our first walk as husband and wife back down the aisle. We floated over the burgundy carpet, past the pews, through the cream-tiled foyer, and out the front doors to our 1989 white Volvo sedan. Family and friends blew bubbles while our mothers cried. It really was a beautiful day.

One that lasted about twenty seconds. Then we had our first married fight.

———

Many of us spent years dreaming about finding the right person, but how much time did we spend dreaming about *being* the right person? I admit, I was far more hung up on what kind of person I was looking for in a mate than what kind of mate I would be. In relationships, it's natural to become focused on the other person as the source of our contentment. Sadly, as time goes on, we can become focused on the other as the source of our discontentment.

Becoming "one flesh" means that both partners bring it all into the marriage bed, the good, the bad, and the ugly. This is why a healthy marriage requires the consistent discipline of pulling a mirror between us and our spouses, so we can reflect on ourselves and what we are bringing into each part of the relationship.

13

The Honeymoon

Just Married" in soap on the windows, tin cans tied to the tailpipe. Loved ones cheering. Bubbles floating from the church sidewalk into the trees.

Our bass player at the time, Steve Goodrum, was the appointed driver for our big exit. The plan was to take a celebratory ride before we returned to the church for photographs. We waved to our well-wishers and slipped into the back seat. I reached up front and patted Steve's arm. "Just circle the church," I told him. "That'll be enough."

"What, no way!" Sarah said. "Ride around the block! Hop on the highway! This is one of the best parts! WE JUST GOT MARRIED!"

I mean, seriously? It's our wedding day. How many of these do we get? —Sarah

I didn't want to cause a ruckus. The thought of drawing attention to ourselves or causing a scene made me a nervous wreck. Typical Matt. Why couldn't I let go? If you ever have license to lay on the horn and drag cans behind your car, it's on your wedding day. We probably could've blasted 95 miles per hour down Glendale Avenue dragging a dumpster full of fireworks and the cops would be like, "Just got married? Carry on!"

Poor Steve. Did he dare choose sides? Down the street for Sarah? Or around the church parking lot for me? In my desperate attempt to avoid conflict with strangers, I had created it with my bride instead.

"Geez, Matt," Sarah said, fire in those sparkling eyes. "Just relax and enjoy the ride."

And that's how our friends and family saw us off in our old white Volvo with "SARAH + MATT" on the windows and soup cans tied to the back. Arguing through fake, plastered smiles in the back seat while Steve sat tight lipped, white knuckling the wheel up front.

And it's all on video! Sure, I was a little disappointed we didn't parade around the streets, and I wished Matt would've danced more at the reception, but he went to a Christian school where dancing wasn't allowed, and I went to a public school where we never held back. I get it now. —Sarah

We were exhausted by the time we reached our hotel, but can you guess the first thing we did? Open cards and count the money! We had both saved sex for our wedding night, so what was a few more minutes of virginity in the grand scheme of things? And come on, we were two broke kids who needed to make sure we had enough gas money to make it to Michigan the next morning. After all the cards were opened, we realized that we had enough cash to make it there and back and even enjoy a couple of steak dinners along the way.

We honeymooned near the Sleeping Bear Dunes of Lake Michigan. Miles of beach and towering bluffs. Lush forests. Sarah and I thought it seemed like a good place for a romantic getaway. Some friends of ours owned a cabin up there, and they were gracious enough to offer it for the week.

Being alone in the woods was pretty romantic at first, but it can be hard for city kids to brave the silence. I may have pulled the old shotgun down a time or two after hearing a suspicious noise outside. "Who's there?" I would yell loudly, awkwardly cocking an unloaded shotgun that I had no clue how to use. I had to prove to my new bride that I could protect her in a dangerous situation, right?

On our second day in the woods, we were already itching for adventure, so Sarah and I drove into Traverse City. We were riding down East Front Street, the main strip, bumper-to-bumper traffic, when a surge of anxiety shot through me and tied my stomach in knots. My IBS had been quiet for years but decided to make a comeback at the worst possible time.

"Pick me up at this same spot," I said, throwing the car door open. "I gotta find a bathroom. Like now."

For a moment Sarah sat clueless, the faint outline of J ST MA R ED still visible on the back window of our Volvo. A little confused, she ran around to the driver side and slid behind the wheel. "Okay, Matt," she said. "Go!"

I hit the sidewalk and ran. There was a flower shop on the corner. "No public bathroom," the lady florist said. El Rodeo Mercado was next door, so I dashed inside.

"No hay baño público," the cashier barked back to my request.

The door jingled behind me as I made tracks down the block. 7 Monks Taproom, Espresso Bay, Truth Seeker Tattoo. At each window, "NO PUBLIC BATHROOM."

Jesus, send a Speedway, I prayed. I scanned the strip for gas pumps and a giant red sign. No Speedway in sight.

Finally, I burst into a small clothing boutique for women. "In your bathroom or on the floor!" I cried. Faces were frozen, eyes wide. I realized I'd said this in the same tone some ski-masked terrorist might demand, *Your money or your life!*

"I need to use the bathroom. Please?" I pleaded with pathetic eyes.

A soft-spoken clerk slowly raised her arm and pointed to a door near the back. "Right over there, sir."

I made it back out front, a few shades paler but overall feeling like a new man. I walked up and down the median, craning my neck for our white 240. *Where were we supposed to meet again?* Just then, I heard the distinct beep of an eighties Volvo horn.

"Are you okay?" Sarah asked when I climbed in.

"I am now," I replied, steering us back onto the strip. Sarah looked at me for a second and then burst out laughing. What could I do but laugh too? Funny how the most awkward, stressful moments can bring us together sometimes.

Bathroom stories may not be the most romantic to share, but it's never the starry-eyed moments of marriage that make us question its meaning. It's the random clashes, catastrophes, and misunderstandings that put love to the test.

The Bible says that God made us a helper so we wouldn't have to face life alone, but joining those two pieces together rarely goes as smoothly as we'd hoped. Because, well, the pieces are broken. Me. You. Him. Her. Us. We're all a mess. When problems arise, that messiness can either push us together or pull us apart.

I used to think that when Genesis tells how that first couple was naked and unashamed, it meant they didn't have any clothes on and were okay with that. But I think it means they were spiritually and emotionally bare too. That's how relationship works best. You let that person see who you really are, faults and all, and you trust that person because love is grace. And grace looks past faults to find the good.

So, you see, this story really is romantic. Not romance like *Fifty Shades* or long moonlit walks on the beach. Real romance is someone who'll drive the car while you hunt for a bathroom because your stomach's in knots. Real love is someone who will laugh because, praise the Lord, you found a toilet on the mean streets of Lake Michigan.

Sarah and I had a lot more laughs that week. We even had a few candlelight dinners and long walks on the beach. But you know what we remember most from that honeymoon? The story we will always tell? Racing around the main drag of Traverse City, trying to find a bathroom. Isn't it strange what moments stay with us?

14

Living the Dream

After much prayer and consideration, Sanctus Real made the decision to sign with a Christian label. We'd formed a good friendship with Chris York at West Main Studios in Franklin, Tennessee, and we signed papers making us official members of the Sparrow Records family. We shook hands, smiled for a picture, and excused ourselves to the studio floor to start recording our first major label release. Between sessions, Sparrow sent us on tour to get the word out.

Sarah and I spent our first year of marriage packed in a Ford conversion van with my bandmates, driving thousands of miles across the United States. We slept in the van through late-night drives and cleaned up in the morning at grocery stores and gas stations along the way. We stayed out on the road working long days into the nights for weeks at a time.

Sarah wanted to be helpful, so she started by working our merchandise table. There wasn't much to earn at the time except for meals, which I'm pretty sure we would've given her anyway. Not lavish meals either. Like some lady from the church brings taco salad (not that there's anything wrong with that) or the dollar menu at McDonald's.

We lived on eight hundred bucks a month. Poverty level, at least by DHS standards. I didn't understand how blessed I was to have a wife who would stand by me under those circumstances. Then again, it's hard to appreciate anything at that age. We were living the dream. Right?

Being on the road playing music was *his* dream. He was *my* dream. So were we living the dream? Yeah, kind of. —Sarah

The road can be a grind, but we had our share of fun seeing the country together. We watched the sunset at Grand Canyon and caught the ocean breeze on late-night drives up the 101. We made sweet memories at Pike Place Market in Seattle, at Mount Rushmore, and down the cobblestone streets of Boston.

In 2002, we were on the road with the Festival Con Dios tour, which some billed as the "Christian Lollapalooza." Twelve alternative Christian acts were packed into a six-and-a-half-hour outdoor concert also featuring X Games–style motorcycle stunts, sumo wrestling, and a mechanical "bungee bull."

The artists and crew dubbed the tour "Festival Con Agua," because it seemed like more often than not we ended up playing our fifteen-minute set in the rain. Many times we would leave soaking wet with no money for a hotel. We'd huddle in the van and try to stay warm as we took turns driving to the next show.

I got five dollars a night to work merchandise. Twelve hours under a flimsy tent in the pounding rain, trying to keep the T-shirts dry. I was happy with that, considering the band wasn't making much more than a hundred dollars a day. —Sarah

Actually, we had to *pay* for our slot on the festival, and they would slip us a daily stipend to help with expenses. Merchandise kept us afloat, so we had to be creative. Our most popular item was a fifteen-dollar green and yellow shirt based on the Subway logo, but often Sarah would try to come up with items on her own for us to sell. She'd buy leather belts at Goodwill, cut them into bracelets, and emboss them with "Sanctus Real." Beaded bracelets were popular, so Sarah crafted some and wrote "SR" on them with a permanent marker.

How corny. I think I sold, like, none of those. What was I think-ing? —Sarah

The good thing about being on the festival is that the venues were feeding us. Sarah was fed up with eating ninety-nine-cent bean burritos from Taco Bell, so she would hoard leftovers. Extra muffins? We'll take those. Shrink-wrapped tray of picked-over cheese and crackers? Why not? Anything to survive and get a few miles farther down the road.

I can remember looking at Sarah late one night with her box full of homemade merch and leftovers to keep my little misfit band going. She was smiling that carefree smile, and I knew the Lord had sent me a full-on Proverbs 31 woman. Industrious. Capable. I mean, check out verse 24: "She makes belted . . . garments and sashes to sell" (NLT).

How about that next verse? "She laughs without fear of the fu-ture" (NLT). Sure, the road was difficult but that's what I remember most. Laughing for hours in that van. —Sarah

15

San Francisco

God is our refuge and strength, an ever-present
help in times of trouble.

—Psalm 46:1, BSB

We were out on the West Coast with a few days off between dates. It was too far back to Toledo, so we figured we might as well stay in San Francisco. We called a long list of churches in the phone book to see if we could find a place to crash. (Remember when we had printed books full of phone numbers in alphabetical order?)

Church after church turned us down. No room in the inn. What I would've given for Twitter or Facebook back then.

What I would've given for a cell phone. The pay phone cost a quarter. Four calls, and there goes your Whopper Jr. —Sarah

Sarah finally got in touch with a church secretary who graciously offered her condo just outside town. The church wouldn't help us, but she agreed to let six scraggly musicians sleep on her floor.

It might have been fun to be stuck in San Francisco if we hadn't been so broke. Still, we figured we could come up with some free/cheap things to do. Someone had the idea to find the actual Tanner home from the opening credits of *Full House,* so we set off across downtown.

We waved to the sea lions at Pier 39 as we sang the *Full House* theme song, then zigzagged up to those iconic steep, narrow streets. "Is that it?" Steve said.

"I don't think it was gray," Mark replied. "Was it?"

Suddenly, a thick smoke billowed over the windshield. It was not the infamous San Francisco fog. It was coming from our van. "Pull over!" Chris shouted.

We piled out, then stood in the street as a tow truck hauled our new van to a repair shop south of town. The mechanic had on a worn blue shirt with his name embroidered on the chest. I can't remember his name, but let's call him Hank. He laid our engine in pieces across the shop floor. "How long you think it'll take?" I asked.

Hank rubbed his grease-stained hands together and gave us a look. I couldn't tell whether he felt sorry for us or was eager to take advantage of a bunch of naive Christians from Ohio. "Gonna take a while, boys," he said.

Determined to persevere, we found the cheapest rental car possible, crammed into it like clowns, and set off to cross one of America's most breathtaking sights. The Golden Gate Bridge. Towering red spans and swaying cables. The bay below us, Pacific Ocean beyond. "Hey, guys?" Chris said. "Is that a . . ."

WHAM!

On one of the busiest bridges in the world, a deer crossed six lanes of traffic and crashed into the side of our rental car. Seriously? We're already missing shows and racking up bills that we can't afford—and now this?

"In this world you will have trouble," the Bible says. No joke. "Take heart! I have overcome the world" (John 16:33, NIV). I wish the Lord would've overcome that deer's urge to play chicken on the bridge while we were crossing it. We found ourselves driving back to the shop in a broken car to check on our broken van.

Turned out our van had a warped cylinder. Apparently, that's really bad. Tour dates awaited in Albuquerque, Phoenix, and Denver, so we traded our deer-dented clown car for a rental van. We played those shows and drove *back* to San Francisco to pick up our van.

We pulled into Hank's shop on a Friday, minutes before he closed for the weekend. Unfortunately, that put us too late to return the rental. We parked by the front door and settled in for a long night.

Somewhere after sundown, I realized we were in the worst part of San Francisco. The rental place was between a seedy-looking pizza joint and one of those discount beer and tobacco places. I could hear the sounds of the street, people drinking and cursing, bottles breaking, police cars and ambulances flying by.

At one point, a brawl broke loose right outside the van. I huddled against the side hull and stayed low. *C'mon, Lord. Please?*

The street noise faded to a rumble. Finally, I drifted off to sleep.

Our repaired van endured its first strenuous drive through the desert and mountains. Exhausted, we finally reunited with the tour. Festival Con Dios was also the first national tour for MercyMe. Their song "I Can Only Imagine" hit the radio while we were out on the road. It exploded first on the Christian charts and then crossed over to pop.

I'll tell you what was hard to imagine—a song about dancing for Jesus playing between Nelly and Nickelback on the Top 40 station. But every now and again, one of those special songs comes into the world, bigger than genres or religious walls.

MercyMe sold sheet music for "I Can Only Imagine" at their merch table. I used to watch them bring in giant stacks, and by the end of the night, every night, they'd be gone. —Sarah

One day after our show, MercyMe's road manager told us that they wanted to talk. *Oh no, what'd I do now?* I thought. *Hope we didn't offend them somehow . . .*

The five of us, road-worn and ragged, barely hanging on, made our way back by where the buses were parked. As the MercyMe guys rounded the corner, I ran up to Bart and practically jumped on him, wrapping my arms around his neck with a squeeze. That was before I knew he wasn't big on bear hugs. Before I could ask what they wanted to talk about, he handed me an envelope.

"What's this?" I asked.

"We're praying for you guys," Bart said. "Hold on."

As we walked away, I opened the envelope. Inside was a thousand dollars, cash.

Thank God for friends and for stacks of sold sheet music.

————

He said to all, "If anyone would come after me, let him deny himself and take up his cross daily and follow me." (Luke 9:23)

When we follow Jesus, we invite Him to reach into the broken pieces of our lives and turn us into something beautiful again. *Broken* and *beautiful* are two words said and sung side by side so often that they can seem cliché, but the power of that paradox never fades because it is at the very heart of God's plan. Those two words dance together in a way that touches our deepest experiences. As we are woven into God's story, we realize that the deepest wells of life's beauty cannot be reached without pain and brokenness, without the mark of the cross upon our own backs.

I'm certainly guilty of hoping that one day God will stop working on me and life will suddenly feel easy. But I know that He loves me too much to stop pushing me to grow up. As I strain under my burdens, God is there, waiting for me to depend solely on Him in my brokenness.

There's a quote in my favorite book, *Wrestling with an Angel* by Greg Lucas, that brings me great comfort in the process.

> I hear religious-minded people say all the time with good intentions, "God will never place a burden on you so heavy that you cannot carry it."
>
> Really?
>
> My experience is that God will place a burden on you so heavy that you cannot possibly carry it alone. He will break your back and your will. He will buckle your legs until you fall flat beneath the crushing weight of your load. All the while He will walk beside you waiting for you to come to the point where you must depend on Him.
>
> "My power is made perfect in your weakness," He says, as we strain under our burden.*

---

* Greg Lucas, *Wrestling with an Angel* (Hudson, OH: Cruciform Press, 2010), 12.

16

Say It Loud

ay It Loud was released on Christmas Eve 2002, and by New Year's Day it had produced the best first week sales of any debut rock record in Sparrow's history. The music was upbeat guitar rock with soaring pop melodies. Positive reviews poured in, and the title track started breaking on Christian Rock radio.

To capitalize on the success of *Say It Loud,* Sparrow sent us on a package tour with Relient K, Pillar, The O. C. Supertones, and a rapper named John Reuben. The See Spot Rock Tour was a smash, sometimes selling out multiple shows in the same day. Sanctus Real played opening slot, kicking it off with "Captain's Chair" and sneaking in some Weezer here and there. Our set was short, but it put us in front of Christian music fans across the United States.

Every other act on See Spot Rock traveled by bus. It was no sweat for them to route the tour through the mountains and across multiple states in one night. Band members slept safely in their bunks while a professional driver navigated them through the night to our next venue.

Sanctus Real? Ford Econoline van, drinking bad coffee at 4 a.m., windows down, trying not to burn up the motor again. Sleeping in the back seat, smelling each other's feet. Twelve-hour drives, double duty, every day and night for a forty-city tour.

Bathroom breaks were tough because we were always running behind. The boys could pee in bottles. Me? My bathroom was the pavement between the back door of the van and the trailer. I had to squat over the trailer hitch in the dark while the boys awkwardly stared in the opposite direction. —Sarah

At one point we took the seats out so we could lay sleeping bags down in the back, but the van sat low and it was a rough ride. Heat and diesel fumes would rise through the floorboards while our skulls rattled with every rut and pothole. Then I'd look at my watch after what felt like forever and realize there were still six more hours to go. What can you do but write a song?

Once we arrived at the venue, we had to set up every bit of stage gear ourselves. Tune our own guitars. Carry our amps. Play early and stay late, hoping to sell enough CDs and T-shirts after the show to make gas money to get to the next town. Load it back up, drive all night again.

It's hard for a man to learn the art of being sensitive to a woman's needs. It's a difficult adjustment even in the privacy of a home. Imagine trying to be newlyweds packed into a small space with your bandmates. It's like Sarah moved into a fifty-square-foot room with me and my three brothers. *Welcome home, honey!*

———

Once the tour was over, Sarah and I moved out of her parents' house and found an apartment. It wasn't much, but we finally had a place of our own. Intimacy wasn't the only thing that was unleashed. All those words we had pent up inside exploded as well. Instead of flourishing in the space and freedom we'd longed for, we began building prison bars with our words. Adding to that stress, our finances were tighter than ever.

One day in a Kroger store, Sarah grabbed a box of Life cereal from the shelf and started eating in the aisle. "Seriously?" I hissed. "What sane person does that?! You can't just rip open a box of cereal before we pay!"

Look, I was hungry. I closed the flap at the register and we paid. No problem. —Sarah

The ride home was tense. She was angry and embarrassed that I called her out in the store. I was angry that Sarah couldn't see why *I* was embarrassed. I defended my stance with some low blow, she let loose and fired back. Matches meet gasoline and . . . *BOOM.*

What is it about married couples fighting in a car that gets so ugly?

––––––––––

It was a rare Sunday off the road. When you work in ministry, it's like you are always in church—but we were thankful for a night where we could simply recharge our spirits without having to sing or set up gear and sell merch.

Calvary had a guest speaker that evening. He shared about God's heart to reach the poor, showing slides of women and children thriving in impoverished countries because of the missionaries our church had supported. I sat there squirming in the pew as he clicked through pictures of precious children half a world away. Heart racing, palms sweating—the church term is *feeling convicted.* I leaned over to Sarah and said, "I think we're supposed to give to this."

"How much?" she asked nervously.

"Six hundred," I whispered, resting my hand on Sarah's knee. My wife is a woman of compassion. I knew she would understand. Keep in mind, our grocery budget was twenty-five dollars a week.

"Are you crazy?" she replied.

A new photograph slid onto the screen. Smiling children living in filth. Raw sewage flowing in the streets. "This was a good day," the missionary said. "Know why they're smiling? They just got their first toothbrush."

Sarah gripped my hand, our wedding bands pressed together, gold against gold. "Okay," she said with a sigh. "Let's do it."

We pledged a hundred bucks a month for six months on top of our 10 percent tithe. I can't tell you that living on less was easy. I cannot tell you that God supernaturally filled our coffee jar back up every morning.

We wrote six straight checks into the missions fund at Calvary. The week after I made the last payment, I got a letter from our health insurance company stating that the company had gone public or private or something along those lines. Long story short, we had somehow become shareholders. Folded inside the letter was a check for just over six hundred dollars.

Have you ever heard of an insurance company paying dividends? I still don't know how that worked. All I know is that God blessed us back with the same amount we had sacrificed. More than that, He blessed us with an assurance that we could trust Him to provide even when things didn't make sense.

———

The point is this: whoever sows sparingly will also reap sparingly, and whoever sows bountifully will also reap bountifully. Each one must give as he has decided in his heart, not reluctantly or under compulsion, for God loves a cheerful giver. (2 Corinthians 9:6–7)

It's easy to see difficult times as roadblocks in our lives. We grow impatient, wanting to pass quickly through adversity. But it's in those times of need that we find an opportunity to stop and discover what God wants to accomplish in us that we can't take credit for ourselves.

Can we rest in chaos and remain generous in spirit, even when our wallets are empty or life has thrown us a curveball? If we become self-focused, we miss the miracles God is doing through our weakness.

17

Fighting the Tide

I see those early years with Sanctus Real like vintage grainy film footage in my mind. Staring out the window as the miles pass by, selfie at the state line, driving in circles trying to find the venue, blinded by spotlights, sweat, guitar necks swaying in unison with lifted hands, crowds singing, signing CDs, Waffle House at 2 a.m., van tires humming on Interstate 80, grab a little sleep, sunrise with my shades on, a million white lines passing beneath the wheels . . .

Same routine, different city. Repeat, repeat, repeat.

But we were making progress with every mile. The See Spot Rock Tour landed on *Pollstar* magazine's Top 50 and *CCM Magazine* readers voted Sanctus Real the "Best New Artist of 2003."

On the heels of this momentum, Sparrow approached the band about contributing a song for an album titled *In the Name of Love: Artists United for Africa.* A portion of the proceeds would go to help the AIDS epidemic there. "Absolutely," we agreed. Then they told us it would be a record full of Christian artists covering the songs of U2.

U2 had an incredible catalog of rock anthems, and the band was doing great things worldwide for the poor and disenfranchised. Bono attended a series of meetings with Christian artists, boldly sharing his faith and encouraging our community to step out and join the cause. But even in 2004 it was cliché for a Christian band to cover U2.

Still, we couldn't deny the opportunity to join acts like Sixpence None the Richer and Jars of Clay, so we linked arms with producer Tedd T to record a cover of "Beautiful Day"—the very song Sarah and I had chosen to celebrate our vows.

I know it sounds crazy but I prayed Sparrow wouldn't pick "Beautiful Day" to be the single. Sometimes God humbles us with His sense of humor. Before we knew it, our version was flying up the Christian Hit Radio (CHR) charts. And that's how a little punk-pop band from Toledo Christian landed our first number one song.

Was it a bittersweet breakthrough? Well, yeah. We'd topped the charts, but I was hoping we could establish ourselves with a song of our own. Again, I had to reorient my priorities. People were dying. If our version of "Beautiful Day" helped support that cause, then it didn't matter if we covered Psalty the Singing Songbook or VeggieTales (spoiler alert).

As it turns out, the success of "Beautiful Day" paved the way for the first single from our forthcoming album, *Fight the Tide*. Radio stations drove "Everything About You" to number one on the Christian Rock chart for six straight weeks. My dream of topping the charts with a song of our own had come true.

The venues were getting bigger, with money trickling in a little better than before. We were finally able to do our first headlining tour. The Fight the Tide Tour was a twenty-five-city tour that featured Hawk Nelson, Seven Places, and Ever Stays Red.

Sanctus Real was still in a van and trailer, but because we were headliners now, we knew we'd need bigger sound and lights and an actual set for our stage.

Hard choice. Do we keep funding our dream? Or provide for our families? We're not high school kids anymore. The machine needs to eat, but our families need to eat too.

The dream mattered more than comfort, so we tried to balance the best we could. Which means we bought new equipment but couldn't afford to pay anyone to run it. Chris's new wife, Dominique, learned to program the light show. Sarah continued to help with merch and lend a hand wherever she could. Everyone busted it to keep the Sanctus Real machine going forward city to city, coast to coast.

All that new gear meant we had to add a rental truck to our convoy. Which meant four people now had to stay awake. Two per vehicle, one to drive and one to kick the driver if he started to nod off. We drove through the night, most every night. We would pull into town just in time to load in, set up gear, sound check, meet the local church and radio dignitaries, do interviews, and play the show.

Meeting people after the performance was an important part of being in Christian music. You get off the stage and go straight to a table or room where you spend time with every single person waiting in line to meet you. The people who love your music—you make them friends, part of the family, part of your story. You listen to their stories. You make them feel special and loved—not because you have to, but because you *want* to.

Often those lingering toward the end of the line would stay the longest. These were the people who had the most difficult stories. How one of our songs carried them through the darkest days or deepest depression. How God spoke to them through our lyrics, and it helped them deal with divorce or death or a crisis of faith.

When someone trusts you with their deepest secrets, you listen like that person is the only person in the world. And they are. But you also know that right over their shoulder are four thousand pounds of gear that you have to tear down and load into the van and truck. You realize there are seven hundred miles between you and the next show and the forecast says you'll be driving through storms. And you know that you will be doing all this again tomorrow. And the next day. And the day after that.

You look at your young wife as she loads another crate into the trailer, exhausted but still smiling, and you thank God for the irrepressible optimism of the young and naive.

Fight the Tide was the right title. Fatigue, ego, hunger of all kinds. We fought it every single day and night.

———

The news came in while we were out on the road. *Fight the Tide* had been nominated for a Dove Award in the category of Modern Rock Album of the Year. The band made a special trip to Nashville. GMA week was huge in those days—an entire week in downtown Nashville, catching up with other bands and artists, meeting new friends, hanging out.

But GMA week wasn't a vacation. Sparrow would schedule interviews for us from five in the morning to ten at night with barely a break to use the bathroom or eat. We tried to divvy up the load, but after five or six hours of "So, how'd you get the name Sanctus Real?" your brain turns to mush. Those last interviewers were probably getting gibberish, but we appreciated every opportunity and did our best to power through. We'd come a long way from passing out CDs on street corners and praying for a break. We were making it, as far as we could tell, and we had to keep our heads in the game.

On April 13, 2005, we put on the fancy clothes we had taken from our last photo shoot. Expensive jeans, boots, and jackets—Sparrow had to buy them for us because we couldn't afford our own. (But the cost came out of future royalties, so we did pay for them in a round-about way.)

We assembled at the Grand Ole Opry House for the 36th Annual Dove Awards. CcCc Winans hosted with Steven Curtis Chapman. Switchfoot won Artist of the Year. Casting Crowns and The Crabb Family won big with four Doves each.

"And the award for Modern Rock Album of the Year goes to . . ." Steven Curtis opened the envelope. Sarah gripped my hand.

". . . Sanctus Real!" CeCe revealed.

We stood behind the podium, thanking God and family, staring past the lights to the sweeping balcony of the Opry House. I tried to enjoy the feeling of something I had wanted for so long. But before we'd even walked offstage, the self-sabotage started in. *No one thinks we deserve this. I mean, do we really?*

Isn't that crazy? You long for something your whole life, and as soon as you get it, the voices start inside your head. *Did we win only because of Sparrow's clout? Does anyone here really like us, or is this just another "pay to play"?*

Ecclesiastes 1. Vanity. Trying to catch the wind. Oversensitive. Overthinking again. The same traits that make me an artist often rob me of its joy. My biggest asset was also in danger of becoming my biggest curse.

18

Surprise

We were winding down the second leg of Festival Con Dios II, rain pouring in sheets. Sarah had started selling glow merchandise for the entire festival. A little more money, a lot more responsibility. It kept her hustling all day.

I went by catering to eat dinner and grab a coffee. Our set was over, and I was bored so I stopped by Sarah's station to say hi.

I was like, *Wow, thanks for bringing me some food and hot coffee. I'm exhausted, cold, and starving out here.* It just felt like Matt didn't give me much thought throughout the day, like I was fending for myself. On my next break, I found him backstage and asked if we could talk in the van. —Sarah

We exchanged a few heated words in the parking lot, but there were some other festival employees nearby so I smoothed it over as we walked toward the van. I was road weary, not in the mood. We sniped back and forth, trying to keep a lid on things. Well, I was trying to keep a lid on it. Sarah kept stirring it up.

"Do we have to talk about this now?" I said, loud enough to turn heads.

"If not now, then when? There's no good time to talk about *my* feelings. We're around other people constantly!"

"Why do you always have to have so many *feelings*?" I said "feelings" like it was some gross social disease and slapped the side of the van. Truth is, I had so many difficult feelings of my own that adding hers to the mix sent me over the edge.

Sarah's eyes caught fire. Audio Adrenaline was cranking out "Some Kind of Zombie" from the stage, the music echoing and distorted from the back. We shouted over the noise. We would have shouted anyway.

"Why are *you* so freaking inconsiderate?" Sarah said.

I threw my hands up. "What are you talking about?!"

"It feels like you go about your business all day long without even considering me, like you're the only person in the world."

"That's not true!"

"Yes. It. *IS!*"

People began to stare. A security guard spoke low into his walkie-talkie. *Is he calling for backup?* Mortified, I pulled Sarah into the van. Now we could start screaming.

"You never think about me!" Sarah said. "It's like I'm just some crew member for your band!"

"Hey, I'm tired too, okay?"

Sarah made a face like biting lemons. "Oh, come on, Matt! You're always chasing this—this *thing*. This *dream*. And the whole time you're chasing it, I'm chasing YOU."

"Oh, please . . ."

"Well, guess what? Your dream's coming true, and God is blessing you, and you're all like, 'Oh, boo-hoo, it's so *hard*. Don't burden me, I've already got so much—'"

"Why do you always have to attack me?" I asked.

"—and I'm just extra baggage," Sarah continued. "Like I oughta keep my mouth shut, sell shirts, and support Matt like a good little wife."

"What? Stop it. You're being all dramatic again."

"Talking about my feelings is not being dramatic! Your inability to handle it is! You never want to talk ABOUT ANYTHING. You ignore me, and you ignore your problems. And you know why?"

I looked away, avoiding her eyes. Sarah moved closer, nose to nose. "You wanna know why, Matt? Because you're selfish."

The fight went on for at least another hour, becoming more toxic. We both said our share of four-letter words. Mark's slipper lay crumpled under the seat. I snatched it up and slammed it against the wall of the van. It felt good. So I did it again.

"Seriously?" said Sarah, unimpressed.

I threw the slipper across the van. It ricocheted off the windshield and knocked over a half-full cup of lemonade Sarah left on the dash. "See?" I grunted, pointing to her mess.

"YOU ARE SUCH A JERK!!!"

"WELL, I DIDN'T START THIS!"

The tour ended, and we headed back to our apartment where we could yell at each other in private. Contempt continued to grow up like weeds, choking out the beauty of what was beautiful between us. Most of the time it would start over some small thing. Sarah was messy. I was too uptight. Our inability to handle tiny problems made them giants instead, and it seemed like Sarah was always in my face, pushing buttons, getting loud.

That same bold personality I admired when we were dating was now a threat. Arguing wasn't a big deal to Sarah. She grew up in a family where everybody spoke their mind. You could be having it out one minute and holding hands around the table saying grace the next.

At the Hammitt house, we pretty much kept it all inside. It wasn't that I wasn't allowed to speak my mind; I think it was just easier not to. Church and family taught me to keep the appearance that everything was under control.

It was late on a Tuesday. I was working on a new song when a scream rang out from the bedroom. Not the usual kind of angry screaming. This was different, like fright or sudden pain. I sprinted down the hall. "What is it? You okay?"

Sarah held a thin plastic strip, eyes glazed.

"What?" I asked. "What's wrong?"

"I'm pregnant."

―――――――――

Character = the ability to meet the demands of reality.
—Dr. Henry Cloud

It's normal for all of us—couples, singles, families, churches—to find ourselves lost in unhealthy cycles of communication and conflict. The stress of life can bring out the worst in us. However, there are greater tragedies in life than conflict itself. For starters, lack of self-awareness and the inability to cope with the demands of reality. Where character is lacking, it becomes difficult to grow closer and stronger in our relationships.

If you desire to grow together in a marriage or a friendship, then you need to face the painful process of change. For years in my marriage, whenever Sarah tried to point out my weaknesses, I would become defensive and turn the tables, pointing out her weakness in return, so I wouldn't have to come face to face with my own. Sarah would admit that she is abrasive in conflict and that needed to change. However, that was no excuse for my unwillingness to choose humility and take what she was saying to heart.

One of the greatest roadblocks to growth in relationships is becoming so focused on the other's failures that you can't see your own.

Why do you see the speck that is in your brother's eye, but do not notice the log that is in your own eye? Or how can you say to your brother, "Let me take the speck out of your eye," when there is the log in your own eye? You hypocrite, first take the log out of your own eye, and then you will see clearly to take the speck out of your brother's eye. (Matthew 7:3–5)

Think About It

1. They called me "Barf King." What about you—was there a nickname(s) from your childhood that felt like a curse? How did that name form the person you were becoming? Do you still carry scars from that time? Yes, sticks and stones can break our bones, and names can crush our hearts.

2. Looking back, I see that I was the anxious, people-pleaser, stuck-in-my-head, avoid-conflict-at-all-costs guy. Sarah was the raw, carefree, unfiltered, charge-the-hill girl. How would you describe yourself in your early, impressionable years? Are you still basically that same person, or have you changed?

3. Think back to the first time you met your spouse. If you're not married, think of the first time you experienced young love. Excitement and butterflies come and go, but they aren't what make healthy relationships last. List the positive attributes of your relationship that are more important than those butterfly feelings.

4. Unrealistic expectations can take a toll on relationships. What are some unrealistic expectations you're holding on to? Consider asking your spouse or someone close to you what they think those might be for you.

5. Conflict. For the most part, how do you handle it? Steer clear of it? Seek it out with enthusiasm? How has that approach served you—well or not so well? Now, you probably come by some of that naturally, but think back to your role models and how/what they taught you about conflict. Are there ways you should adjust your approach?

6. Sarah and I love to think back on times God sent someone to help us when we were in need. Consider the times others have helped you. Is there an opportunity for you to encourage someone else who needs it right now?

What About Us?

19

Our First Arrow

Like arrows in the hands of a warrior are children
born in one's youth.

—Psalm 127:4, NIV

What began with a blood-curdling scream ended in a tearful embrace. "It's okay, it's okay," I assured her. "I am *so* happy." Sarah was just afraid. We couldn't even get marriage right, so how could we be good parents?

"Now that it's inside, I have to push it out!" Those words mixed with her wincing expression made me want to laugh out loud. I tried to hold it back, but our tears turned to laughter as we shared a moment of celebration over the gift of our first child.

Sarah was determined to stay out on the road and help the band for as long as possible. There were times during the show when I would gaze out into the crowd and catch a glimpse of her same glowing smile, knowing that our child would soon feel that same warmth. I can still picture that Sanctus Real hoodie hugging the sides of her round belly. I loved to stand behind her, wrap my arms around her, and cradle her baby bump with my hands. The smell of her hair and softness of her cheek nuzzled back against mine. Those were precious times.

I enjoyed those moments, but the flip side was that Sarah was on her feet all day, setting up merch booths and selling CDs. Eating Taco Bell at midnight, grabbing what sleep she could get in the van. One night we were sleeping between the cargo door and the bench seat of our van, bouncing around for the entire sixteen-hour drive. Somewhere around 4 a.m., Sarah realized this was not a healthy lifestyle for a soon-to-be mom.

By this time, we'd bought a house back in Perrysburg, so Sarah went home to rest. She picked up a few hours a week at a local hair salon, putting her cosmetology license to work. Even though our marriage could be stormy, it was tough for me with her gone.

As demand for the band was growing, so was my longing to be home. We would be out for two or three weeks at a time with only a day or two at home between dates. If we went on a long trip out West for example, we had to play as many shows as possible to pay the bills.

It was always a predicament to see that I'd be out for ten days, off for two, and then back out for another week. Do I try to go home for those two days? Because buying a plane ticket would have wiped out a week's salary. I spent most of my off days in mall parking lots and coffee shops, soul searching, missing Sarah, and wishing I were home.

———

Sarah and I did our best to stay connected. I finally had a cell phone, but it wasn't smart by any means. It was an old Motorola with a tiny screen and no capability to text. The only thing I could count on was digital solitaire.

At least I could call my pregnant wife back home. Sometimes. The reception back then was really spotty. We used to carry those brochures from Sprint around, studying them to find the next place we should be able to find service. *Should* being the key word. There were plenty of times we would pull off onto the side of the road near a town with good towers and take a few minutes for everyone to call loved ones before driving back off into no-man's-land.

Also, there was the fuzzy math of cell phone charges. You got some free minutes depending on your plan and then time at a discount. Roaming costs were astronomical. As you can imagine, bands roam a lot.

The worst was getting into an argument during those precious moments of cell time. That took a toll both emotionally *and* financially. You're ranting and pacing the church sanctuary trying to get reception bars—doing your best to be discreet because it's not good to have fans see the nice Christian singer yelling into his phone. It was all too easy to start the infamous rumor that your favorite Christian band really isn't so "Christian" after all.

We had been fighting a lot more since Sarah left the road. It seemed like she always needed something more from me than I was able to give. I get it—she's back home alone, pregnant, needing my help, struggling to keep up with the bills and the maintenance of a house. But it's not like I was on vacation. Playing music was my job. I was lonely too. Couldn't she see I was doing all this for God? For us?

Intentional or not, Sarah knew exactly how to push my buttons. I'd hold it all in, becoming more and more defensive until I blew up. We were constantly trying to get on the same page, and it was as if the page kept turning, and we would get stuck in that loop of arguing and yelling, each trying to prove our point.

Strange thing is, those fights seemed so crucial and vicious in the moment, and I can't remember the details of any of them now. Not one. There's a big lesson in that alone.

In the early morning hours of February 22, 2006, the band was headed north, passing through New Mexico for a show in Denver. Except for a few small towns, it was all desert and mountain range.

It was a time before our lives got so hyperconnected and taken over by screens. Unless you were close to a city, there was no reception. You could drive and think and talk to God, oblivious of everything else in the world.

My water broke two weeks early. I am dialing frantically. *Jesus, please give Matt bars.* —Sarah

Sarah finally got a call through as we made it to the southern rim of Albuquerque. She was on her way to the hospital with her dad. My first baby was about to be born, and I was fifteen hundred miles from home.

You couldn't book a flight on a flip phone. You could barely make a call. Thank God, Chris spotted a sign for Albuquerque International Sunport, and as it turns out, we were only minutes away.

"Drop me at the airport," I told my bandmates. "I don't know what you guys are gonna do about the show, but I've got to get back home."

Wrestling my suitcase from the trailer, I ran into the abandoned airport. The ticket counter was closed for the night. I bedded down on a nearby bench so I could be first in line at the counter as soon as they opened the next day. I set the alarm on my phone, prayed, and actually slept pretty soundly. Once you've spent the night on the floor of a hot diesel van, a quiet airport feels five-star.

The next morning, I headed straight for the counter and paid the absolute, most asinine amount of money one can pay for a last-minute plane ticket home. Something like seven hundred bucks on my credit card. I didn't care. Whatever it took to get me back to Sarah before our first child was born.

I landed in Toledo, raced straight to the hospital, and made it just in time to wash up and throw on some scrubs. Not two hours later, Emmerson Mae Hammitt was born. "Here you go, Dad," the doctor said. "Wanna cut the cord?"

Talk of blood alone has always made me faint, but come on, Sarah had just pushed a child out of her body. "Um, yeah," I replied. I put my thumb and index finger through those cold scissors and squeezed. In that moment it all became real. For nine months Sarah held our child in her belly, feeling her heartbeat, her kick. Being a parent became a reality to me, too, as I received my daughter into my arms.

Emmy was quiet and wide eyed, taking it all in. Stretching her neck up, licking her lips, already curious about the world. We were stuck in a moment, taking in the wonder of holding and being held. I remember thinking how strange it was that this was my daughter, to feel that much responsibility for a person I did not yet know. What I would have given to never leave home again.

But I felt I had no choice. It was time to go back on the road.

20

After the Wind

Then I considered all that my hands had done and
the toil I had expended in doing it, and behold, all
was vanity and a striving after wind.

—ECCLESIASTES 2:11

The Christian Rock genre was at the peak of popularity in the mid-2000s. Back then, there were large numbers of fans turning out for bands that, like us, had no real presence on the AC (Adult Contemporary) radio charts. People would rush the front of the stage and stay on their feet the entire show, jumping up and down in unison and singing every word with no restraint.

The only part that made me uncomfortable was when a crowd would get out of control. I never understood why—it wasn't like we were a hard rock or metal band. But I guess these were youth group kids with pent-up energy, finding their one place to let off steam.

I did my best to keep things calm, but sometimes pastors and parents would get upset. I'd have to stop the music and do that crowd-out-of-control announcement. "Okay, hold on. Everybody take one step back. See this kid down here? He's just trying to have a good time, and he got hurt. Let's respect each other and keep it a good time. Lift each other up, instead of pushing each other down. Okay?"

Sometimes the pastor would take the stage before our concerts to lay down the guidelines. *(Seriously pastoral voice)* "All right, guys and girls. I want everyone to have fun tonight, but we won't be able to unless you follow a few simple rules . . ." The first rule was always "no moshing." Yep, *moshing*—that was a thing. Maybe I'm too old to know if it still is. I always felt a little bad for the poor pastor having to give a stern warning about moshing and skanking. Man, those were the days.

I visited a big music festival recently, and everybody was watching passively or staring at a phone. Any bit of response had to be prompted by the band. It made me thankful I got to play live during an exciting time in Christian music history, before recorded and live music were at people's fingertips. They weren't skipping through endless singles on streaming services for free or watching full-on rock 'n' roll productions at church on Sunday morning. People were still hungry to experience music back then, and we felt that every time we played.

With a new baby at home, I felt the pressure to step things up. Finances were only a small part of my concern. What if I missed Emmy taking her first steps while I was on the other side of the country playing a show? Is Daddy just that tall guy who visits now and then?

But playing shows was what paid for diapers and baby food. And it wasn't just a job—we believed it was our God-given calling. Then again, I didn't want to be a stranger to my own child. The tension between home and the road was growing.

I wanted Matt with us for birthdays and holidays, to be there for Emmy's first words and steps. Reasonable requests were always followed by the fear that people would peg me as "Yoko." —Sarah

I wanted to draw boundaries between my career and family life, but how? Everything becomes negotiable when the doors to opportunity are finally starting to crack open. Can we do your birthday the Tuesday before I leave? What if we celebrate Easter when I get back? If Emmy starts crawling, will you video it so we can watch it together when I get home?

Regardless of my good intentions, this is the message I was sending: work is first; Sarah and family always come second. They're the ones who have to adjust. Everything has to revolve around me and my crazy schedule.

I was doing my best to juggle career and family. Wasn't every family man doing that? Besides, I was just one guy in the band. How could I cancel a string of concerts so I could be there to blow out candles on a cake?

There was no easy fix. I didn't want to step on anybody's toes, didn't want to upset the applecart. Never wanted to tell anyone *no*. Management, the fans, other bands, the label, the blogger requesting an interview. I was just that anxious kid from a small town with a big dream. And big dreams require big sacrifices. Lose focus, lose your hunger, and the industry will sweep you to the side. A thousand people are waiting for your spot and are more than willing to work around the clock.

You keep chasing the carrot. One more show. One more interview. One more special trip. Just one more, this one's really important. All your time and efforts are spent on others while your family gets whatever crumbs remain.

———————

The life of mortals is like grass,

   they flourish like a flower of the field;

the wind blows over it and it is gone,

   and its place remembers it no more. (Psalm 103:15–16, NIV)

There's something I understand about my life now. I always knew it, but it was hard to believe when I was at the center of my dream. I hope you take it into your heart. Here it is.

It will all go on without you.

People may appreciate you while your gifts are on display, and hopefully they'll speak fondly of you in the end. But the world will keep spinning after you're gone.

I've heard this said by different people in many different ways, but I'll give it a try in my own words. When it comes to climbing the ladder of fame, wealth, and career, there are a thousand people behind you ready and waiting to take your place. Most of them would never be sorry to see you go. Every reader may take something different from this book, but if you're a husband or father, I desperately hope you won't let this truth pass by without taking it into your heart. Your wife has one husband and your children have one father. No one can take your place. God created you to do that job in a special way that only you can do. Without you there is a painful void.

21

Not All Right

After the momentum we felt from *Fight the Tide,* Sparrow was eager for us to start a new album. Stay gone too long, and people will move on.

We were working with a producer named Christopher Stevens at the time. He had just moved to Nashville from Eugene, Oregon, and had a makeshift studio in his garage while he was getting settled in. Pushing hard without a break was weighing on us, and he could feel it.

Song ideas were running low compared with previous albums, and our inspiration was nearing empty. We all wanted to be home with our families. But the machine never sleeps, so we'd traveled to Music City to make another record instead.

I played Stevens a rough idea the band and I had worked up called "I'll Be Fine." It was that bland sort of overly optimistic Christian song. You know, like, *life is hard, but with a little faith everything will be okay.*

But there was an angst between Chris Rohman's guitar riff and the melody that screamed for something more. Stevens asked us what would happen if we stopped pretending to be doing better than we really were. What if we put aside the fear of being too unpolished and let the truth be heard instead?

Revitalized by honesty, we poured ourselves into new lyrics for the song. We even called in our friend Doug McKelvey, whose prose and prayers could crack the hardest of hearts. Together, we found the right words to express the way we felt.

If you want the truth, I need to confess
I'm not alright

None of us were all right. Mark had his first baby about the same time I did, but on the day his son was born, his dad was two floors below in the same hospital dying from cancer.

Mark's dad was so excited about his first grandson. And just as baby Benjamin is born, he has to start saying goodbye? How do you square that away with the goodness of God we sing about? And do we sing some happy song where everything works out by the chorus, or do we sing about a deeper, more mature faith, one that wrestles with all the things we cannot resolve?

What ministers to people most? False hope or honest doubt? Our band name literally meant "authentic, honest songs of praise." What comes from my heart that I can call true?

Throughout this same season, my grandmother's Parkinson's disease was progressing. We moved her into the same hospice Mark's dad was in.

Grandma died. Mark's dad died. Steve left the band and went through a difficult divorce. Sarah and I were fighting all the time. But we still had to go onstage and preach hope, even if we felt overwhelmed and hopeless.

We wanted that tension to be felt in our new record. Honest. Broken. More mature. But we knew it was a risk.

To our surprise, Sparrow embraced the song and gave us a substantial budget to make a video for "I'm Not Alright." The band flew out to a patch of desert north of Hollywood and spent sunrise to stars performing the song on a stretch of abandoned highway that cut through the sand.

They set up the performance shots on a crossroads. It was an undeniable metaphor for everything we were feeling. The desert. The heat. The sepia-toned landscape. We were at a crossroads mentally, spiritually, emotionally, musically, financially. In the video, two cars barrel toward the band as we stand there flailing away, oblivious to the coming danger.

"I'm Not Alright" became Sanctus Real's sixth straight number one song. The video was picked up by MTV and *The Face of Love* debuted at number five on *Billboard*'s Heatseekers chart.

We were honest about how messed up we felt, and instead of turning away, Christian listeners embraced it. Apparently, we weren't the only ones who needed an anthem of authenticity.

———

The only way we'll last forever is broken together.
—Casting Crowns

You can't be attached to the idea of utopia if you actually want to be changed by love. Spiritual transformation is a lifelong process that requires seeing ourselves and others for who we really are. The permission to speak freely and honestly is priceless, knowing our faith and relationships will become stronger as we engage in conversations that would be easier and perhaps safer to avoid.

Visiting evangelical communities around the world, I get the feeling that a lot of people still feel the need to present a more acceptable version of themselves, even to friends. Maybe it's fear of judgment or simply the belief that no one actually wants to be burdened with their real problems. The human spirit can't thrive without a safe place to discover the beauty of being genuinely loved and known by God and others. Christian community should be a place not only to build up the best in one another but also speak loving truth when needed . . . without offense. That's hard.

Without authentic community, people burn out from faking it. Acceptance becomes an idol when it can't be reality. Sadly, many wounded Christians run off into the open arms of a community that will receive them exactly as they are but is devoid of healthy friends who challenge them to grow in life and faith.

22

Something Heavenly

The more you make this world about you,
the more miserable you will be.

—MATT CHANDLER

It was late one night back in Ohio. Clean and dirty clothes were piled in the laundry room, mixed in one giant heap. Trash cans overflowing, dishes stacked in the sink, baby toys strewn from one end of our house to the other.

All the upkeep of a home fell on Sarah while I was gone. Diaper changes, plumbing disasters, air-conditioning repairs, grocery shopping, bill paying, having to be both Mom and Daddy too. When I was home, she needed my help, but I was a zombie from the road, exhausted, restless, sleepwalking through the day, wired at night. Still, I roused myself and ravaged through the house in a cleaning frenzy, steaming contempt.

"You're being a jerk, Matt," she said.

"A jerk? I didn't even say anything!" I sneered. "I could show you what a real jerk looks like."

"You say plenty without words, stomping around, sighing like a big baby. You're never here, and when you come home, you act like this?"

"Fine! You want me to use words? This house is a disaster! I can't believe you let it go like this. I don't even want to know what it looks like when I'm not home to clean up after your mess!"

Sarah gave me that look, the one that's a mix of hurt, sadness, anger, disappointment, and despair. I was used to it by now. I had looks of my own. We kept at it, both of us hissing, trading verbal punches, playing defense. Sarah finally stormed off to bed. "Don't follow me!" she said. "I want to be alone."

I paced the kitchen, rehearsing all the reasons I was right, muttering under my breath. *What does she expect me to do? Not work? Shouldn't home be a place where I can recharge and rest?* Eventually, my self-righteous raging ran out of steam. I slipped down the hall and checked in on Emmy as she was sleeping, snuggled safely in her bed. It was peaceful, and I sure needed peace, so I stood in the doorway and tried to let it soak in.

Some say you can never truly comprehend the love of God until you have children. Until you watch the rise and fall of their breath as they lie sleeping and know that you would climb any mountain, take any bullet, fight any giant to keep them safe and warm.

But few of us will ever have to step in front of an actual bullet or fight a nine-foot Goliath to save our kids. Sarah had a point. The mountain to climb wasn't so much laundry or dishes as it was me. Because the next morning, I'd be leaving again.

My daughter deserved better—a father who wasn't gone all the time. She needed me there to kiss her chubby cheeks in the morning, push her on that yellow swing in the backyard, wrap my arms around her mother while she was watching, giving her the assurance that her home was safe and secure.

I hoped that in the long run she'd understand her dad was trying to do something of eternal value. I traveled the country telling people about a God who loves us, a good Father who is ever present to help us in times of trouble. But if that's what a good father does, then how could I justify being never present and emotionally unavailable?

It's easier for Christians to paint a happy picture, like we never really struggle with anxiety, depression, or doubt. Or if we do struggle, it's a quick lapse that's easily corrected by a few simple adjustments to our spiritual lives. I'm here to tell the truth, though. Every part of my life felt like it was falling apart. I dreaded walking out that door again. I just wanted to find some local nine-to-five job, be home for coffee in the mornings and dinner at night. Or did I?

I took my guitar to Emmy's playroom and started to fingerpick my feelings in chords. I asked God to open a way out, to let me be home. But instead, I felt His hand on my shoulder, holding me in place. The whisper in my soul said, *I am not done with you yet.*

I felt angry, but what could I do? I could fight it, or I could surrender. I took all those twisted feelings and did the one thing I knew I was good at. I poured them into a song.

It's hard to surrender to what I can't see,
but I'm giving in to something heavenly.
—"Whatever You're Doing (Something Heavenly)"

It's been thirteen years since my oldest, Emmy, was born. That was when I first began trying to reconcile my life as a traveling musician with the kind of husband and father that I desired to be. The song

"Whatever You're Doing (Something Heavenly)" came from those burning questions of how to balance touring with my family life. I felt God assure me that I was meant to continue with the band, and I remained obedient to His calling. However, I never stopped wrestling with the reality that my life on the road, away from my family, had been the root of many struggles for me.

I'm not proud to admit that I selfishly blamed those struggles on Sarah at times, as if the unrest I felt on the road had more to do with her weaknesses than mine. When tensions arose from me being away, I wanted to believe she was simply projecting displaced emotions toward me, distracting me from being fully engaged in our ministry on the road. In reality, it was my failure to lead properly that left her needing more in those times, both spiritually and emotionally. I'm grateful that she never checked out on me, even when I was pouring my best into other people. She never gave up on pursuing the kind of marriage that she knew God desired us to have.

By God's grace, I can now see that the primary responsibility lies with me.

23

Signs

Sanctus Real was becoming a core artist in the industry. It was bizarre to pull into a strange town and see a giant picture of the band wrapped around some Christian radio station's Kia Sorento. They even put our picture on the Renaissance Hotel sky bridge during GMA week.

I remember the first time the band and I stood side by side in Target, staring at a shelf of our CDs. I knew that, like me, Chris and Mark were thinking about bashing around in that basement all those years back, eating Cheez Whiz and playing Tom Petty songs. Little things, like seeing our CD in a store, was a big deal in light of our humble beginnings.

By the end of 2006, Sanctus Real had become the CHR format's most played artist. More money was coming in, but we were still firmly middle class. Our yearly touring salary was about forty thousand dollars. Don't get me wrong; I'm grateful. I just want to put to rest the rumor that having a music video and songs on the radio makes you rock-star rich.

It's not much financial reward for being away from home over two hundred days per year. One night in the van, I started doing the math out of curiosity. I discovered my wages were something like twenty-five cents an hour. I could've made a better living working the window at Mickey D's.

Many of my musician friends had settled into solid positions with churches. Salary, benefits. Security. Home for dinner every night. You still get to do what you love.

Often, some pastor would pull me to the side and say something like, "Hey, brother, if you ever get tired of the road, we'd sure love for you to come be our worship leader. We'll take real good care of you and your family." The offers were starting to get tempting, but could I really even consider such options and still be in God's plan?

You know what's always been a mystery to me? We all feel some sort of divine calling in our heart that's a bit different than a dream. We feel the *something more* that we were born for, but sometimes a calling feels like the wind. Which direction is it taking me? And tell me, what's the line between God's sovereignty and our free will? If I should choose to use my gifts in a different context—say in a church instead of on the road—could I still live out my calling?

First Thessalonians 5:16–18 says, "Rejoice always, pray without ceasing, give thanks in all circumstances; for this is the will of God in Christ Jesus for you." Does this mean that regardless of vocation, we can still live out God's will moment to moment, openhanded, with a prayerful and thankful heart?

For all the mistakes I made, despite my fears and all my anxious wavering, at the end of the day, I still felt like playing in Sanctus Real was where God wanted me to be. I just wished I didn't have to be so torn between the journey and the call.

The band was out on some lost highway across America. I was driving, hypnotized by the distance. Thinking about a song. Thinking about In-N-Out Burger. *Mmm, Double-Double. Grilled bun. Animal-style fries (topped with cheese, chopped grilled onions, and the special sauce).*

My cell dinged with a text from Sarah. I glanced at it. Picture attached. Emmy holding a sign. *Oh, okay. Cute.*

The sign was tiny. I blew it up until the print became clear. At first, I didn't get it. Then the words sank in. I let off the gas and pulled to the side of the road.

"Matt?" Mark's sleepy voice came from the back. "Y'okay?"

Eyes wide, heart pounding. I read Emmy's sign again.

"I'M A BIG SISTER!"

24

Push, Baby, Push

M att, I don't know how I'm going to do this," Sarah confessed. "You're already gone so much. How are we gonna make it with two?"

I wasn't naive to how difficult it was going to be, but I truly believed that familiar passage in Romans, that God would work it all for good. "The Lord will make a way," I assured her.

Cue the touring montage again: Tires on asphalt, fast-food wrappers scattered in the van, the band looking a little more haggard this time. Mic check one, check two, tuning guitars, hustling to finish before the rain. Another festival/church/theater/auditorium full of kids. "Hello, Cleveland, we're Sanctus Real!" *Matt, we're in Kentucky.* "Hello, Kentucky!"

Sleeping on floors, writing songs, cutting tracks for another new CD. Pacing church parking lots, fighting with Sarah on the phone as her belly grows rounder by the day. Faster and faster, the footage blurs. Suddenly, I'm rushing through the hospital, flying through sliding doors. Gown up, gloves on, I squeeze her hand. *Push, baby. Push.*

———

After five glorious days at home with new baby Claire, I had to get on a plane to England for the band's first show across the pond. We played a festival at a theme park in Manchester with the band Delirious? and planned to see the local sites once we were done.

I stopped back at the hotel room to clean up a bit. A message was waiting at the desk. MR. MATT HAMMITT: CALL HOME IMMEDIATELY.

Toledo is five hours behind England. Cell phones didn't work overseas back then. Even if they would have, it's not like we could have afforded the minutes. After dialing a complex series of numbers from the landline, the phone finally rang through to the States. Sarah answered, the line filled with static. I knew immediately that something was very wrong.

"They think Claire has meningitis," Sarah said, her voice breaking. "Matt, they're telling me she could die."

Our precious daughter had needed a spinal tap and extensive blood work. But the hospital botched the labs so they had to repeat everything again. It was chaos back home. Sarah was in the middle of it with a two-year-old child and a sick baby while I was halfway across the world.

I hung up, feeling helpless. Somehow I got my things together and made my way to the airport. Another baby, another desperate plane ride home. It's a nine-hour flight from the United Kingdom to the United States. I had plenty of time to wrestle with God.

Did He send me? Or was I just like a thousand other kids who grew up dreaming of playing in a band, traveling the world, and seeing our name on posters and videos and CDs? Was I using ministry to justify my selfish dreams? Is the call of God on my life really to play upbeat songs about Jesus? Or is God's primary purpose for me to be right there close to support my family in difficult times?

I wrestled back and forth the whole way, thirty-three thousand feet above the Atlantic Ocean. I'm so glad David wrote the Psalms to show us what honest prayer looks like, to let us know that we can come just as we are, our messy, doubtful, moody, confused selves.

By the time my plane touched down, Claire's condition had improved. Further tests showed it wasn't meningitis, just an infection that the doctors were treating with antibiotics. She would get better and things would be okay. I thanked God that baby Claire was healthy but couldn't shake the frustration.

It felt like there was always something pulling at me, always some crisis I couldn't afford. When I was on the road, I missed home. It was hard to enjoy home because the road was calling. I always felt scattered, missing the moment, skipping like a rock across the water.

My bandmates were supportive, but they needed me too. When Mark had a family crisis, we told him to take as much time as he needed. We sent him home and hired a drummer to fill in for shows. When Chris and Dominique had their first baby, we told him the same thing. "Go home, man. Drink it in. Take as long as you need."

Chris helped us find a replacement, and we kept rolling on. Sanctus Real was not the same without Mark or Chris, and sure, the chemistry was not complete—but the show went on.

But I was the singer. If I sat out, the machine stopped. I'm not saying the show was all about me or that I was more important than my bandmates. I'm just saying that's how the mechanics of our band worked.

An anxious mind amplifies every potential problem in its time. If there was grace, I couldn't see it. The thought that kept me conflicted was this: *If I don't go, the band suffers. If I go, my family suffers.*

Everything is on me.

25

Sarah's Song

It was two thirty on a quiet Tuesday afternoon. The kids were down for a nap. HGTV was playing in the den, the umpteenth replay of a stylish midwestern couple searching for the house of their dreams. I had just gotten home that morning, and as usual, the bus was scheduled to head back out Thursday night.

I should have been spending time with Sarah, but instead I was distant, detached, orbiting some new song idea in my head. She appeared in the doorway. I glanced over. "What's up?"

"Matt," she said. "We need to talk."

I followed her into the dining room and took a seat across the table from her. "You're here." Sarah began, gesturing toward the walls of our home. She locked eyes with me before continuing. "But you're not *here*."

I stared down at the table, feeling the guilt, not defending myself for a change.

"Your heart and mind are always chasing something—but it's not us. When I express my needs, it's too much for you. Instead of trying to understand, you get defensive. I'm lonely when you're not here, and I'm still lonely when you are. I married you to have a partner, someone to do life with. But it's like I'm doing *our* life, and you're off doing yours. There are days when it seems like you're not even part of this family. I want you to take ownership of our spiritual and emotional well-being. I need you to be our leader."

Chest tight, stomach in knots. I twisted my wedding band in a slow circle around my finger as she spoke. "I just can't be the strong one anymore, holding everything together for all of us." Sarah's voice cracked. She took a deep breath. "I need you to be strong for me too."

I could no longer deny the truth. Our marriage was in crisis. I nodded back as Sarah talked about the criticism, the apathy, all my passive-aggressive swipes. We had argued about this a thousand times before. I had developed a few survival tactics for Sarah's lectures, like rehearsing comebacks in my mind or rolling my eyes when she was being overly dramatic. This time I just sat there, listening. I knew she was right. I had wanted to give her my best but didn't know how under the circumstances.

As she poured her heart out, I didn't hear the angry tone I had expected. I heard only sadness and saw a wife who had finally had enough.

I sang about grace but hadn't learned to live it. Mostly because I struggled to receive it for myself. I preached to thousands about unconditional love, but my relationship with Sarah could be volatile, moody, with tons of strings attached. I had failed to make her feel loved and known. But then again, did I feel accepted?

Sarah stood and vanished down the hall, leaving me to contemplate her words.

I finally began to understand how lonely her life must be. In an effort to follow my calling, driven to pursue a dream, wanting to build a ministry, I had neglected some of her deepest needs. I thought about balance, unsure if there was really such a thing in life. But if there was,

I wasn't anywhere close to finding it. I was distant to the ones who needed me most, and my constant efforts to avoid confrontation wound up creating it instead.

On a shelf beside the table were photographs from our life. Our children, our parents. Sarah and me on our wedding day. I picked up the photo, wiping away the dust, studying our faces.

In that photo, Sarah was glowing, filled with hope and expectations for our future. It crushed me to see the contrast between the radiant face of the woman I married and the broken one that I lived with now. Worst part? I still wasn't sure how to fix it. James 1:5 says if anyone lacks wisdom and asks God with faith, He will give it to you.

God give me wisdom, I prayed. *If I'm going to lead her, I need You to lead me.*

My whole life I had carried the desire to be a great man. To live up to my highest calling as a husband, father, and friend. In that moment I realized that good intentions are worthless until they become actions, based upon the needs of the people you love. Not what you *think* they need, but what they *actually* need.

I came face to face with a harsh reality. The man I thought I was and the man Sarah perceived me to be were two very different people. I had been defining myself by intentions and internal dialogue rather than actions. Sarah didn't need to hear any more excuses. She longed for the evidence that I was receiving her into my heart and cherishing her as the gift that she was to me.

As I sat there staring at our picture, the words she spoke played over through my mind. *Matt, I need you to step up. For me. For our children. Be the man of your house. Lead this family.*

Tears welled up again. There was so much emotion in that room I felt like my heart would crack in two and crumble into ashes. But I knew exactly what to do with a tangle of emotions. I knew how to take brokenness and disappointment and pain and turn it into something beautiful.

Using her own phrases—how she needed me to stand up and fight, to be there for our family, to stop chasing dreams and give her the love I had promised on our wedding day—I put her heart's cry into a song. It was rough, but there was an ache in the melody that rang true.

> Show me you're willing to fight
> That I'm still the love of your life
> —"Lead Me"

I called Sarah in and sang it for her. She listened, then gave me a courteous smile with a nod. It was clear that she needed more than a song.

The opposite of love isn't anger, it's indifference. —Tim Keller

Women often ask me what Sarah said to me the day I wrote "Lead Me." I think they're hoping for a magic key to unlock a place in their husband's heart that they haven't been able to reach. But remembering Sarah's exact words has been difficult. She doesn't remember them either. And she would say it's because we had a version of that conversation a thousand times before I actually took her words to heart.

One of the most important things people need to know is that our marriage didn't change overnight. Taking her words to heart was just the first step in an ongoing process that I like to call "The Lead Me Journey." For me, it's the journey of moving from a man of good intentions to a man of action as the spiritual leader in my home.

A few years ago, I asked Sarah to clearly articulate her need to me again, so I could give a more thoughtful answer about what it is she wanted and what I've been working to give her. Sarah said, "I want you to be in control, confidently steering our ship. Intentional about our relationship, emotionally strong and mentally present." I immediately thought of the verse in James, about a double-minded man, being tossed back and forth on the waves. That was me before I started to take consistent, measurable steps toward real change with God's help.

26

Surrender

Success can sometimes be just as disconcerting and
frightening as failure, especially when you have
questions about your own unworthiness and abilities.

—DON HENLEY

I t was a big moment, one long overdue. Sanctus Real would finally
move out of our van and into a tour bus. Problem was, we had to buy
one. In Nashville, there are a ton of buses to lease. Buses everywhere.
Not so much in Ohio.

We finally found a well-worn Prevost that had been previously
owned by the Barenaked Ladies. (As in the band, Barenaked Ladies.)
We couldn't afford a driver, so Chris got his CDL license. On late
nights and long stretches of highway, I'd offer to slide behind the wheel
and give him a break, but he was hesitant. Driving on the open road
did something for Chris's soul. I think part of it had to do with his
desire to take care of everyone and keep us safe out there. I admired that
about him.

Canada to Texarkana, state fairgrounds and an endless string of
first, second, and third Baptist churches. We were touring to promote

our latest record, *We Need Each Other,* but crowds were getting smaller as the industry began turning its attention toward a new class of artists.

Sanctus Real was no longer the hot young buzz band. We had worked hard to be an act that drew a steady crowd. Suddenly, it was two hundred people. One hundred, sometimes. We had to play more shows to make the same amount of money. The smaller the crowd, the greater my insecurity would be. It wasn't just a matter of confidence; I was fearful that I wouldn't be able to provide financially for my family anymore. That increased the pressure to write another hit, to be a better front man, to work even harder and do even more.

Ironically enough, Sparrow released "Whatever You're Doing (Something Heavenly)" as a single, and it was getting decent play on the radio. I would sing that song to half-full seats and kids who seemed less than interested. *Okay, Jesus, it's over, right? Can I leave now?*

I could still sense God's hand on me, and in that still, small place, He would speak. *I am not done with you yet.*

We got booked to play the LifeLight Festival, a three-day concert in Sioux Falls, South Dakota. Switchfoot and Michael W. Smith headlined, and nearly three hundred thousand people turned out for the event. Even though Sanctus Real was a little farther down on the bill, it was nice to play in front of a larger crowd.

I stood in the wings as our friends in Tenth Avenue North played their set. Mike Donehey was a singer/songwriter/guitarist like me. Except Mike seemed to love performing. I believe he had even been to acting school. He was confident and charismatic in ways I could never dream of being.

I watched Mike onstage, and it all looked so natural and easy for him. *Why was he made that way and not me?* I thought. *If this is what I'm called to do, why does it feel so difficult?*

It was just me and Mike backstage after the show. "I dunno, man," I told him, staring at my feet, kicking rocks. "Seems like you were born for this. You have so much confidence, and I still feel so unsure."

"You're great at what you do, Matt," Mike offered graciously. "God just gave us different gifts."

"Thanks, man, that means a lot. I just can't seem to get comfortable in my own skin. It's hard to see people like you who have so much confidence."

"Pride is most recognized when we rely on our own abilities, like 'look at me, how good I am,'" Mike said. "But there's another kind of pride that disguises itself in humility. That pride is like, 'Woe is me; I suck.' In both cases, we're basically saying, 'It's all about me.'"

Wow. That was a brass-knuckle punch to the chest. How many of my actions and attitudes were driven by anxiety or insecurity instead of service to God? What if what I thought was insecurity was actually pride in disguise? What if being humble was just camouflage for a massive preoccupation with my own feelings?

Reality check number two. I was beginning to feel crushed from both sides. I felt like a boxer in the ring of life taking some bout-winning hits from the truth. The pain of spiritual and emotional growth can feel more real than physical pain at times. Your whole inside aches as your new self is ripped away from the old. Sanctification can really beat the hell out of you, both literally and metaphorically.

———

It was a typical day of touring in the Midwest. Long stretches of cornfields led us to a high school in the absolute middle of nowhere. No posters, no promotion. We loaded our gear into the fieldhouse and did our regular sound check. The sun went down as we kept an eye on the windows, watching for cars. Show time came, and we walked from our tour bus to the stage. Programmed lights flashing. PA buzzing with power. Fifteen people in the seats. Maybe.

I used to preach passionately how every sacrifice for the gospel was worth it, even if you only reached one heart. When you work in ministry, you hear sayings like that every time the crowd is sparse or the money comes up short or things don't go as planned.

I strummed through the intro to "Whatever You're Doing," thinking about my wife and babies back home doing life without me. I looked out at a handful of half-bored people who were checking their phones and thought to myself, *This is the last time I will ever play this song. In fact, it's the last time I'll ever stand on a stage. I'm over it. Done.*

David Nasser was traveling with us, as our speaker on the tour. Good guy, good heart. One afternoon, I caught a ride into town with him. I needed to get out of the bus. Clear my head.

The sky was bright blue. It was cool out, and the sun warmed my face through the car window. "I think it's over," I told him. "I can't do this anymore."

David nodded, flipping his blinker to change lanes. "If you need to take a break, take one, Matt," he replied. "You don't have to be done."

We drove a few miles without speaking as I mulled over David's words. They made sense, even if I didn't want them to. Maybe I just needed rest. Even Jesus needed rest. Burnout is common in ministry. Doesn't mean you need to quit. "Look at Third Day," David offered. "Mac took a break, but it didn't mean the band had to break up."

But Sanctus Real wasn't like some other bands who enjoyed financial security. Every show was essential to our survival. There was no re-serve, no savings account to pay our bills if the wheels stopped turning.

We pulled off the interstate to get coffee and call home. I'm sure Sarah was tired of hearing it, but I had to let off steam. Smaller crowds, less pay, less support. More doubt, more bills, more pressure to produce.

Sarah was quieter than usual. "Something wrong?" I asked.

The line went silent. Somehow, in that pause, I knew the words that were coming before they arrived. But when she finally spoke, I was still surprised.

27

Pieces of a Real Heart

We weren't trying to get pregnant. Then again, we weren't really trying *not* to get pregnant either. I mean, we knew how it worked. I was excited and terrified at the same time. Every two years, new Sanctus Real record. Every two years, new Hammitt baby. Life kept getting crazier. —Sarah

In March 2010, Sanctus Real put out our fourth major-label record, *Pieces of a Real Heart*. The cover featured a heart made of jagged patchwork pieces, and the songs were more reflective this time, struggling through the confusion and fragility of life, talking about the place where faith and reality collide.

We began to experiment with our sound and leaned into our producer, Chris Stevens, inviting him to play more keys. We even introduced banjo and glockenspiel into some of our tracks. Not so much garage-y punk-pop. We were growing up, having babies. Chris and Mark's wives were also expecting, making eight kids between us by the fall. I suppose less distortion and more acoustic instruments were a better fit for us in that season of life.

We wanted to take the songwriting further, deeper, to be more honest about our struggles. Sarah's dining room table song made it onto the record. At first, I didn't draw attention to it because it felt too personal. Sarah and I were still working on our issues, and I had zero interest in being that vulnerable onstage.

The demo somehow made it to Peter York, president of Sparrow. He had a gut feeling we needed to finish it, so Chris and I set up a writing session with our friend Jason Ingram.

Jason had already listened to the rough version of my song. Though it wasn't much, he heard the same potential Peter did, the heart and tears I'd poured out of my life. We set out to take the song higher, handling every phrase and nuance with care. When our session came to an end, Jason did something that I hadn't seen him do before. "Guys, I think we should pray over this song," he said. "It has the potential to change a lot of lives. Let's pray that it goes further than we ever imagined."

A month after *Pieces of a Real Heart* was released, Sarah and I went for our nineteen-week ultrasound. We heard Lisa Williams, one of the K-LOVE morning hosts, hyping our appointment live as we drove down Reynolds Road. We'd seen her at a show the night before, and she thought it'd be fun to update listeners after we discovered whether our new baby was a girl or boy.

While Lisa teased listeners to stay tuned for our big gender reveal, we were holding Emmy's hands, swinging her between us as we walked into our obstetrician's office in Toledo.

Emmy was at that age when she talked all the time, everything new, everything so exciting. She'd been having a recurring dream. "I dreamed about my brother again last night!" Emmy had told Sarah a few weeks before.

"Wow, okay," Sarah had responded. "But how do you know you have a brother?"

"We were onstage singing. But he dies, Mom. He dies." She'd said it in that casual four-year-old way, not yet capable of the weight behind the words. It wasn't the first time Emmy had this dream. It had happened twice before, first when she was two years old, at an age when she was just learning to articulate emotions and thoughts. It seemed so strange when Emmy told us that her brother would die. How did our toddler understand what death was?

Up in the doctor's office, they called us back to the exam room with Bridget, the same tech who had done all our ultrasounds before. "I saw you when you were still in your mommy's belly," she told Emmy.

"Really?" Emmy said, amazed.

"Yep. I was the first to know you were a girl," she said. "What are you hoping for?"

"I want a brother!" Emmy replied, as she gazed in wonder at the fuzzy white blob wiggling on the screen.

Sarah whispered into Bridget's ear. "She has this weird dream about a brother who dies."

Bridget nodded as she moved the probe across Sarah's abdomen. The room got quiet. Bridget's face grew serious. "I can't get good pictures," she said.

The ultrasound took much longer than usual. She finished up and led us to wait for Krystal, Sarah's OB/GYN. We sat in silence. Krystal entered, sorrow in her eyes. "I have some bad news," she began. "Something is wrong with your baby's heart."

The air left the room. We were devastated. "Is he going to die?" Sarah finally asked.

There was a long pause. "I don't know," Krystal replied.

We walked out and back across the parking lot, still numb. I climbed into the car and turned the ignition key. Back then, we still used our car's CD player. I waited for the disc to start spinning, for a song to break the silence. But instead, the player made a strange noise, *ERROR* flashing across the screen.

Our CD player had never malfunctioned before. I tried again. *ERROR*. I hit the radio button and heard the opening riff of a familiar song. "Hold My Heart" by Tenth Avenue North began to play.

I listened to the voice of my old friend Mike, reassuring me of something I desperately needed to hear in that moment. He hadn't written it about a child's heart, but that's the way God meant for us to hear it that morning. A gentle yet bold reminder that He was with us. Holding us. Holding our unborn baby boy. As the song played, I reached for Sarah's hand and we began to cry.

Once the song was over, I shifted into reverse and drove away. When I hit the CD button again, it worked just fine.

I crawled into Emmy's bed that night and asked about her dream. "How old is your brother when he dies?"

"As big as you and Daddy, Mom," she said. "We're all onstage singing." —Sarah

28

Psalm 139

You created my inmost being;

you knit me together in my mother's womb.

I praise you because I am fearfully and wonderfully made.

—PSALM 139:13–14, NIV

From that moment on, our life was consumed with doctors, specialists, and Google searches. Our baby had a rare congenital heart defect with a name that echoes its complexity. Hypoplastic left heart syndrome, or HLHS for short.

For babies born with HLHS, the left side of the heart is severely underdeveloped and can't pump blood, so the right side must supply both the lungs and the body. Without immediate surgery, the condition is fatal. As the medical staff performed more tests, they told us that in addition to HLHS, our baby was missing a finger, had bowel issues relating to Down syndrome, and that he may have trisomy 19, which was described as "incompatible with life."

"You should consider terminating the pregnancy," one specialist in Toledo advised.

In fact, he implied it would be selfish of us to choose otherwise. His claim? Abortion would be the best option for both the baby and us.

We were angry and brokenhearted. I would not let my son's life slip through our fingers like a simple grain of sand in the universe. Sarah and I believe that every life is a gift from God, meant to be lived and celebrated, so we decided then to name our baby boy Bowen, meaning "small, victorious one." We claimed the words of Psalm 139 as if they were his own.

> For you formed Bowen's inward parts;
>   you knitted him together in his mother's womb.
> I praise you, for Bowen is fearfully and wonderfully made.
> Wonderful are your works;
>   my soul knows it very well.
> Bowen's frame was not hidden from you,
> when he was being made in secret,
>   intricately woven in the depths of the earth.
> Your eyes see his unformed substance;
> in your book are written, every one of them,
>   the days that were formed for Bowen.

Bowen's heart might be small, but we knew that, life or death, we would celebrate his victorious story. His life would not be in vain.

I headed back out to the road to promote *Pieces of a Real Heart*. My brothers in the band supported me the best they knew how, and I did my best to support Sarah in light of the latest diagnosis and barrage of coming medical appointments. I feared how we would handle the expenses, imagining the piles of medical bills that I'd witnessed swallow people's lives. I needed to work, but it was harder than ever to leave Sarah and the kids behind.

Pieces of a Real Heart began to feel prophetic as we played the new songs, words that were written before Bowen was even conceived. Sarah wept as they played in the background at home. It was hard to hold back the tears while standing on church platforms singing, pleading lyrics from our album: "Jesus, keep my heart alive" and "You can make a weak heart live forever."

Even the album cover seemed foretelling, a heart torn in pieces and pasted back together again. That's what the doctors told us would happen. Bowen would have open heart surgery soon after birth to try to correct what was broken. It would be scary enough for an adult like me to have open heart surgery—how could I wrap my head around the idea of doctors taking a scalpel to my newborn son?

Sarah and I handled our crisis in different ways. She immersed herself in medical literature, studying online, searching every term, learning everything she could about Bowen's condition, the treatment, the outcomes, the drugs, the surgeries, the expectations for life.

I turned to my own grieving process—journaling, writing songs, and starting a blog titled *Bowen's Heart* to update family and friends. Not only did I pour my words out in our blog, I poured them out in song, creating a collection of psalms and lullabies that I could play at Bowen's bedside once he was born. I wanted my voice to wash over my son, for him to hear his father, prayerful, earnest, and tender. I also wanted to hear my own voice singing back to Sarah and me as we sat at his bedside in that hospital, reminding us of God's faithfulness when we reached the verge of abandoning faith.

As the days passed, we prayed, cried, studied, and felt the anguish of not knowing whether or not our child would live or die. We connected with other parents who let us know we were not the only ones struggling to understand. We met with an endless array of medical professionals who performed tests and tried to help us prepare for what lay ahead.

———

As a musician, I found it amazing to watch the ultrasound machine turn sound into sight, allowing the pediatric cardiologist to measure the size and blood flow of Bowen's heart while he was still inside the womb. We sat in that dark room, staring intently at the screen, looking for a sign, praying to be told that blood had somehow started flowing to the left side of that tiny heart. After a detailed examination, the cardiologist informed us that Bowen's heart remained unchanged.

One, two, three ultrasounds. Once again, I watched the tech measure Bowen's arms and legs, counting fingers and toes, chasing him around for a good shot of everything she needed the doctor to see.

Our doctor looked over the images and said that everything looked okay despite Bowen's diagnosis. He then reiterated what he'd told us before, making it clear that the chances of Bowen having a chromosomal anomaly were higher because of his heart defect. He offered to perform an amniocentesis, and although the test could tell with nearly 99 percent accuracy whether Bowen had other defects, we politely declined.

The chances of having a baby with HLHS are about one in

twenty-five hundred while the chances of having a miscarriage due to an amniocentesis is one in four hundred. Sarah and I would still feel blessed to be parents, even if our child was born with Down syndrome or any other illness.

Even in the worst case, if a test deemed Bowen to be "incompatible with life," Sarah and I would never question carrying our son to term and cherishing every second he was in our arms. But if we did an amniocentesis and Bowen ended up being the one in four hundred babies who died, we would not be able to live with that choice.

The next set of decisions we faced was where to deliver and who would be Bowen's surgeon. After consulting with physicians, we made tentative plans to deliver in Toledo and transfer Bowen to C. S. Mott Children's Hospital in Michigan for his first open heart surgery with Dr. Edward Bove.

On May 1, I posted a list of things on *Bowen's Heart* that I never want to forget:

- Staring at that first ultrasound while holding Emmy's hand. Watching her face light up when she found out her wish for a little brother had come true.
- When the CD player in the car wouldn't work, but a touch of the radio button brought up "Hold My Heart." Thanks, God. I needed that.
- On the phone with Sarah after a show. "I want to buy our baby boy clothes," she told me, her voice trembling. "But I'm scared he'll never wear them."
- Coming home a few days later to find a pile of boy clothes in our living room.
- Buying my first gift for Bowen, a little red race car from Genius Jones in Boca Raton.

- Over two hundred emails of encouragement after sharing our story on K-LOVE and The Current FM.
- The look in Sarah's eyes. Only God knows my heart better. I'm honored to share this struggle with someone as wonderful as she is.
- The new level of compassion I feel for the sick and dying.
- The peace of knowing God in the midst of suffering.
- Gratitude for grace and every small moment.

29

Lead Me

Sparrow released "Lead Me" as the second single from *Pieces of a Real Heart*. So much for not wanting to air our dirty laundry. You know what they say: if you want to make God laugh, tell him your plans (Proverbs 19:21).

In one sense, "Lead Me" was a song about all my failures, about Sarah calling me out to be the spiritual leader, to be a better man. That's very personal stuff, and for a while, every time I performed the song, I felt like I was back in fifth grade standing in my underwear before my classmates.

But "Lead Me" slowly began to catch on, and I could tell something was connecting with the audience. For me, it was coming from a deeper place spiritually, more vulnerable than I'd ever been before. Sarah and the kids needed me more than ever, and I sang it as a desperate prayer.

Every time I played "Lead Me," I had to examine myself and ask, *What kind of man am I? Not yesterday or tomorrow, but today.* I wanted to be a better spouse and father, but if I was truly going to lead my family, I needed God to lead *me.*

While I was dealing with my pain through songwriting and jour-naling, Sarah was burying herself in the medical process 24-7. We tried to reach out to each other, but the urgent can easily eclipse the essential. There was just so much going on between Bowen and the band.

"Lead Me" began to take off on the radio, bringing attention back to Sanctus Real. More bookings, more interviews and appearances. At-tendance increased at our shows. People began to pick up on Bowen's story, and we received encouragement and prayer from all over the world. Praise reports, prayers, notes from adults born with HLHS who were alive and well. That hope and support carried us through the low-est moments. But even as I was singing about fighting for love, Sarah and I continued to drift apart.

I read an article that claimed 85 percent of couples who have a critically ill child eventually divorce. Once you're there, you under-stand. It's just so hard. —Sarah

––––––––––

Time passed and Bowen's arrival was upon us. I tried to prepare myself by studying his condition, but seeing the facts in black and white stirred every anxious tendency within me. Even with the advances, 30 to 50 percent of babies born with HLHS don't make it to age five.

I grew up believing in healing, in miracles, in the power of mustard seed faith to move mountains, in asking without doubt, lest you be like a wave of the sea blown and tossed by the winds. I prayed hard for heal-ing but also for the strength to accept our circumstances. I didn't want to get my hopes up only to be crushed.

Sanctus Real was touring through Oklahoma and Texas. I sang "Lead Me" night after night, praying for strength, asking God to please not let Sarah go into labor while I was so far away.

A week or so out from her due date, she posted this to *Bowen's Heart:*

About seven years before I had kids, I bought this adorable lion costume for Halloween. It didn't work for the girls. It was made for a boy, size twelve months. I got it out when we learned we were pregnant with Bowen. It's in his cradle next to his stocking cap and tiny stuffed alligator. I look at it every single day.

Bowen will be fourteen months when Halloween comes again. I tell myself that he'll be here, toddling around in that costume. That he'll be healthy and happy, and if you didn't know any better, you'd never believe he was living with half a heart. His big sisters will help him from door to door, and he'll be a sticky mess from munching on all that candy. I'll let him have as much as he wants. Then there's the other part of myself that tells me not to get my hopes up, to accept that Bowen might not be here to wear that costume next year. That thought wrecks me. It's a struggle to open my heart fully, knowing it might get broken. But in the end, I know I won't be able to resist.

————

We know that for those who love God all things work together for good, for those who are called according to his purpose. (Romans 8:28)

Have you ever wondered why God created a pathway to pain and death in the garden of Eden? The Bible reveals God's eternal plan for all that is broken to be made new again, but why did He let us be broken in the first place? I don't have the answers to those ever-pressing questions about sickness, sin, and suffering in the world, but I'm coming to peace with what I don't know.

What I *do* know is that suffering is intertwined in the story of every living thing. And I truly believe that no one is hurt by our brokenness as much as God Himself. I personally have faith that He put that tree in the garden for good and glorious reasons beyond my scope of understanding.

30

Welcome, Baby Bowen

Bowen Matthew Hammitt was born on September 9, 2010, at 7:59 p.m. at the University of Michigan Women's Hospital. "Seven pounds, seven ounces," the nurse reported to Sarah and me.

They let us hold Bowen for a brief moment. I remember his bare skin against Sarah's chest, tears and sweat mixed. The joy of holding our perfect, precious gift was sweet bliss, but it ended quickly as the nurses whisked Bowen to C. S. Mott Children's Hospital and upstairs to PCTU (Pediatric Cardiothoracic ICU).

Then they wheeled Sarah into recovery and worked to get the feeling back in her legs, due to her epidural. She looked over to me, teeth clenched, eyes blazing. "Get me back to my baby," she said.

I felt like a caged animal. I was desperate for Bowen to feel me, see me, hear my voice. I wanted him to know he had a fierce mama who would fight alongside him the entire way. —Sarah

Bowen's first open heart surgery was scheduled in five days, the first of three life-threatening procedures he would have to endure to try to repair his heart. For a time, we soaked in all the joys of being proud parents of a brand-new baby. Bowen was so sweet and tiny. We couldn't stop staring in wonder at the sight of our little boy wrapped in a blue striped blanket, snuggled next to his stuffed alligator, wearing the cap that his great-grandmother Gloria knit together with so much love and prayer.

We took a picture of Bowen in the incubator, his skin smooth. We ran our fingers over the soft, perfect skin in the center of his chest, knowing he would soon have a scar zippered down it. As I placed my hand over his heart, I prayed for God to heal him, to help us face this trial, to guide Dr. Bove's hands and bless our broken hearts too.

Emmy and Claire came up to meet Bowen for the first time. After expressing how cute and cool her new brother was, Emmy said, "Can we go to the playground now?" Claire concurred.

I set up a Bose SoundDock at Bowen's bedside and connected it to my iPod. I had it loaded with the songs I'd written for him, along with a few others from artists that had touched our hearts. We politely urged his nurses to keep those songs playing around the clock, even through the night. I believe music has the ability to heal, and I wanted songs of worship, love, and truth relentlessly washing over my son.

Bowen didn't look fragile, but he was. His oxygen saturation levels were dropping and eventually they had to intubate. Truth is, he wasn't doing very well at all. On September 14 we watched them roll his bed away to prep Bowen for surgery.

I was sick to my stomach, my head was spinning, and I was scared. But I kept saying to myself, *God is good, no matter what.*
—Sarah

Time crawled as we waited in that awful, anxious nowhere land of hospital waiting rooms. We reminded ourselves that Dr. Bove had performed nearly ten thousand pediatric surgeries, and Bowen was in good hands. But those thousands of surgeries were not our son.

"The procedure was a success," Dr. Bove told us when he finally pushed through the doors into the room. "But he's not out of the woods yet. The next twenty-four hours will be crucial."

Bowen remained in critical condition. More doctors came to consult. The room buzzed with an edgy tension, specialists checking monitors, brows furrowed, shaking their heads. I once heard a musician say that sirens and hospital monitors sound off in augmented fourths, also known as "the devil's tone" in medieval times. In that moment, I was convinced it was true.

The atmosphere turned dire. Bove pulled us to the side. "Listen, his body is not liking this," he said, in that no-nonsense tone of surgeons. "We're starting to get concerned."

We watched and waited. Hours passed into the night as fatigue set deep. We were staying at the Ronald McDonald House across the street from the hospital, but Sarah refused to leave PCTU. Her feet were swollen twice their normal size, and it had been days since either of us had slept. The nurses kept reminding us of the long road ahead, that we'd need to rest to be strong.

Sarah finally agreed to go back to our room and try to sleep, but only after making a deal with the charge nurse that she could call in for regular progress reports. We climbed into bed and set an alarm to ring every hour on the hour. The first went off at 1 a.m. Sarah called over. The nurse told her that Bowen was stable. At two, the alarm woke us again. "Everything's okay," the nurse assured Sarah. "Try to get some rest." At 2:13 a.m., the phone rang. "Come quick," the charge nurse said. "We've started compressions."

31

2:13 A.M.

You are my hiding place;

 you will protect me from trouble

 and surround me with songs of deliverance.

—PSALM 32:7, NIV

Panic pulled Sarah from the fog. *He's dying,* she realized.

"Matt!" she shouted. "Get up!"

I threw on a shirt and staggered out the door. The hospital was across the street, but it was too far to run. We jumped in the car, and I floored it, parking sideways by the hospital door, scrambling into the elevator and up to the fifth floor. We raced down the hallway and into PCTU. Doctors and nurses hovered over Bowen's bed, pulling at tubes, calling codes. We ran to the foot of his bed, and they parted to let us step in.

He looked like a rag doll, so lifeless and gray. All I could do was stare down at the bed sheets, hold Bowen's toes, and pull his blanket close to my face. —Sarah

Bowen was in cardiac arrest, his chest still open from surgery, wires streaming from his arms and legs, a tube drooping out of the side of his mouth. A nurse worked feverishly, her fingers around Bowen's heart, pumping it to keep him alive as the on-call surgeon raced toward the floor.

The speaker at Bowen's bedside blared loudly, Audrey Assad's ethereal voice filling the room. The music swept over us as time began to crawl. Shiny balloons floating over incubators, brightly colored elephants on the wall, tubes and wires snaking to beeping monitors. So much blood. Audrey's voice soared above the noise, "I am restless, I'm restless, 'til I rest in You." It all seemed like some tragic scene from a movie, and I couldn't help but think, *This is the way that God has chosen to take our son.*

I stood there frozen as the doctors shouted, planning Bowen's funeral in my mind, wondering how we would tell the girls so they wouldn't blame God, trying to imagine how Matt and I could possibly survive. —Sarah

For all my efforts to process the pain, I had still stuffed everything deep down. My method of coping and keeping hope alive had been to believe and focus only on the best. In that moment, I realized that hope wasn't enough to save a life. I wasn't prepared for a truth so difficult as that.

As "Restless" faded, I reached to cue the song I had written months before for this very moment. I picked up Bowen's stuffed alligator and held it tight. I wrapped my arms around Sarah, buried my head in the back of her sweatshirt and began to weep.

They pulled us into a waiting room next door. A glass pane was all that stood between me and my dying son. I collapsed into a rocking chair, clutching Bowen's alligator to my chest, trying to breathe. It was over. I knew it. We were just waiting for them to call the time of death.

Sarah sat across from me, dazed with grief. I called out to God in desperation. *Father, if this is even a fraction of the pain You felt when You gave us Your only Son . . . we thank You for letting Jesus die on the cross. Put into motion the redemptive and healing power of Your Son's death and resurrection to spare the life of ours.*

And then we waited, each minute feeling like an eternity. The same nurse who had called that morning rushed in to tell us that Bowen's heart was beating again.

The doctors had successfully placed him on life support. As Sarah appealed to the nurses for answers, I stumbled to the foot of Bowen's bed and watched the surgeon reach into my baby's chest, making one last check of his heart before leaving for the night. He covered Bowen's chest and looked over to me with smiling eyes.

"Hey, Dad," he said. "You've still got a kid in there."

32

Love Is an Awesome Mess

I can't give you half my heart and pray He
makes you whole.

—FROM THE SONG "ALL OF ME"

There are a lot of risks for a child on life support: bleeding out, blood clots, damage to the brain. We didn't get much sleep, staying close to keep watch.

After thirty-six hours, the medical staff successfully weaned Bowen off life support. It was hard to believe it had become somewhat normal for me to peer down through that window in my son's chest and watch his beating heart.

A friend told me during this time that I had seen too much, but I realized that maybe I wasn't seeing enough. Struggle breaks you and it hurts. But it was also deepening my faith and stirring me to be a better man. As I stared into Bowen's eyes, my face only inches from his chest, I thought, *This love is an awesome mess.*

As I mentioned before, I'm not the first to paint the tensions of life in these sorts of terms. We often find redemption revealed where the worst of life and the best of hope collide. God allows us to know great pain so we can trade it for greater purpose. You can be angry and bitter when difficulties come, or you can let them teach and change you for the good. I was determined that Bowen's pain would have a purpose.

———

Bowen spent a couple of weeks in ICU before a step down to moderate care. He slowly got stronger, but it was still touch and go with complications arising from day to day. Fever. Infection. Heavy sweats. Hypoglycemia.

I was feeling pretty discouraged one afternoon when the staff rolled a contraption into the moderate care room. It looked like those cases that delivery guys carry to keep the pizza warm, except bigger and it had windows on the sides. The nurses opened the lid, pulled out a beautiful baby girl and placed her in a bed not far from ours.

After some time had passed, her father walked over. "Are you Matt?" he asked, extending his hand toward mine. "My name's Jake. We've been following your blog."

Jake pulled a worn piece of paper from his pocket and unfolded it. Printed on the sheet were the words to a song I had written for Bowen called "Trust," about trusting God in the questions, doubt, and darkness.

Jake's daughter, Paislyn, was also born with a heart defect and was awaiting surgery. Jake told me that he and his wife had been holding on to the lyrics of "Trust" as a reminder of God's faithfulness. In doing so, Jake reminded *me* of God's faithfulness.

Later that night, I wrote this entry in my journal.

The hospital has become a strange comfort to me. It reminds
me of a church, where sick and hurting people come to find
hope. I've developed a sense of community here. Not only
have I found comfort in others, but also in comforting
others. I'm not just singing about the place where heaven
and earth collide; I'm living in it. I'm not just looking at
need from a distance; I'm holding it by the hands, looking
it in the eyes. The greatest comfort I have is that in the
midst of suffering, I have come to find something greater
than hope. I have found the assurance that life is more than
just a body.

"My flesh and my heart may fail, but God is the strength
of my heart and my portion forever" (Psalm 73:26).

———

Bowen's small blood sugar problem became a massive roadblock to recovery as he began to suffer strokes and seizures. His heart was healing,
but C. S. Mott's team of endocrinologists could not get his sugar under
control.

"We don't understand what's happening," they told us. "Children's
Hospital of Philadelphia is the leader in endocrine problems. If this
doesn't improve, I'm afraid we're going to have to life-flight you out to
CHOP."

Sarah dove back into her research and discovered that a small per-
centage of patients experience hypoglycemic side effects with the medication Bowen was on. She presented this evidence and begged the staff
to consider changing his meds. We didn't want to pretend to know

better than our doctors, but it felt as if we were watching our son slowly melt away.

One night, after his meds, Bowen's sugar dropped to 17, and he suffered yet another stroke. It was beginning to look like he might die from complications with his blood sugar rather than his heart.

Finally, to appease me, the doctors agreed to try a different medication. I told them if there was no change, they could life-flight us to CHOP. They switched it, and within twenty-four hours, he began to stabilize. —Sarah

Thank God, Sarah was willing to rock the boat. With the blood-sugar crisis in check for the moment, we finally stepped down a level of care to the floor where the endocrinologists did genetic testing for hyperinsulinism. If the results came back positive, we would still have to go to CHOP for surgery on his pancreas. I joked that I'd have to start a blog called *Bowen's Pancreas* because, well, sometimes in a really dark place you have to try to lighten up a bit.

I can't tell you there weren't times when my faith was weak. The lows were low, and there were days when I couldn't bring myself to read my Bible or pray. The hardest was the kids who didn't make it. I never knew what to say to parents who had to leave the hospital empty handed. Anything I could come up with felt so trite.

What would I want someone to say to me in such a time? I think I've figured out that the best thing to say is nothing. Maybe, "I'm so sorry." A hug or the squeeze of a hand. None of those quotes about everything happening for a reason or how heaven must've needed another angel. Just be willing to bear witness to great pain without clichés; just weep with those who weep.

They sat with him on the ground seven days and seven nights,
and no one spoke a word to him, for they saw that his suffering
was very great. (Job 2:13)

———————

There were a few more setbacks along the way. The incision on Bowen's
sternum became infected, and they had to open it again. Then they had
to redo the wires they used to hold him together. We still had to watch
his sugars closely, but as time passed, he continued to improve.

The medical staff doted on Bowen, bringing him toys, dressing
him in the University of Michigan colors. (Go Wolverines!) Let me tell
you, it takes a special kind of person to care for sick infants, and we are
so grateful for those God sent to walk with us through this trying time.
They saved Bowen's life and in doing so saved ours too.

Children's Hospital is a heartbreaking place. But there is a light and
a hope that is impossible to describe. In the midst of all that suffering,
in the middle of wound vacs and IVs and tiny babies born with broken
hearts, God was with us. Nobody was debating theology or fighting
about politics. We were all desperate for God and for our children to
live.

Late one night, with Bowen and Sarah sleeping, I wrote these words:

I cannot explain this, but in the darkest time of my life, I am
consumed by Glory. These difficult days are some of the closest
to God I have ever experienced.

33

Home for the Holidays

After you have suffered a little while, the God of all
grace, who has called you to his eternal glory in
Christ, will himself restore, confirm, strengthen, and
establish you.

—1 PETER 5:10

It was a week shy of Thanksgiving when we got the news that Bowen could go home. Sarah and I had to attend emergency response classes, CPR classes, NG (nasogastric) feeding-tube classes. Trying to get a newborn baby to let you stick a tube up his nose and down his throat? That was not fun.

Two days before the discharge, we got a call from *ABC World News Tonight* asking if they could do a story. I know we prayed God would use Bowen's life, but we were beyond burned out. We didn't want a national news crew trailing us home. But Sarah and I prayed about it and knew that's exactly what we were supposed to do.

The team from ABC met us at the hospital and followed along as we prepared for discharge, cameras in our faces as the nurses tried to brief us on really important details of Bowen's care. We swaddled him in a car seat and checked everything four or five times. The hospital staff gave Bowen a standing ovation as we carried him outside. We secured him carefully in our SUV and headed back toward Ohio with film crew in tow.

Emmy and Claire waited in the front yard, clinging to their stuffed animals, signs taped to the garage saying, "WELCOME HOME, BOWEN." We brought him inside and wrapped up filming. The crew couldn't have been nicer, gracious with every step. (Google "Baby Bowen ABC News" to see the video.)

And then they left. After over two months in the hospital, we were finally home. Just me, Sarah, the girls, and Bowen.

I was happy and so thankful to God. But I was scared too. Really scared. —Sarah

It felt like we'd been handed an atomic bomb encased in delicate glass. They unplugged this super-fragile, medically challenged child from his giant rack of monitors, handed him over—and now we were on our own.

We had asked God to help us accept reality and this was it: puke, clean up, puke, bath, puke, laundry. We washed more clothes in thirty-six hours than we had in thirty-six days. Emmy saw our neighbor in the yard. "Hey, Bowen's home!" she called over. "He's puking though!"

Sterilizing an endless array of tubes and syringes. Sixteen medications, five times a day, and a continuous supply of special baby formula to keep his blood sugar stabilized. I offered to stay up with Bowen, but Sarah refused to leave his side.

I was afraid he'd aspirate, so I would sleep next to him all night,
every night. He woke up every hour and made the most awful noises
as he began to throw up. —Sarah

Every time Bowen would cry, his NG tube would start to come
out. It felt cruel to hold him down and wrestle it back in, but it had to
be done. It was nonstop bomb defusing. Our insurance company as-
sessed us for night nurse assistance, but we didn't qualify. We had some
help from family and friends, but it was still so much.

World News Tonight aired our story the night before Thanksgiving, and the Toledo newspaper, the *Blade,* ran a sweet article that also
managed to slip in a mention of Claire's sparkling pink shoes. *Bowen's
Heart* got so much traffic that it broke the blog. Maybe even the entire
internet.

We gathered with family for dinner on Thanksgiving Day. I looked
over my house full of kinfolk, taking it all in. I don't know what we
would have done without our parents to watch over the girls, without
neighbors and friends, and without our two little girls who brought us
so much joy.

I don't know what I would have done without Sarah, who was so
bold and courageous in the most devastating of times. I was striving to
lead our family but always felt I was learning so much from her. She
fought tirelessly for our children and for us. My heart was full of thank-
fulness for her.

As I looked at my baby boy that Thanksgiving, I think I felt more
gratitude than I ever had in my life. Bowen soaked it all in, wide eyed
and smiling. If it weren't for that thin white tube in his nose, you'd have
never even known he was sick.

———

Christmas was around the corner. For nearly a month we'd been struggling to keep Bowen's feeding tube in place. One night he managed to
pull it out, and we couldn't get it back in. It was midnight and we hit a
breaking point, both of us in tears.

"You know what?" Sarah said. "Leave it out. I'm done with it."

"Really?" I replied with a losing-my-mind sort of smile.

"I'll feed him and check his sugar every hour," Sarah said with a
determined tone.

From that day on, Bowen began to gain weight and get health-
ier. He stopped throwing up, slept better, and even started smiling
and cooing at us all day long. —Sarah

34

Pain and Purpose

The week Bowen was born, "Lead Me" went to number one and stayed there for nine straight weeks —the entire time he was in the hospital—giving Sanctus Real our biggest song ever.

Stories began to pour in of how "Lead Me" was impacting marriages and stirring men to action. I needed the encouragement and was thankful that the song's success brought a lot of attention to Bowen in his time of need. Christian radio stations around the world were playing "Lead Me" and telling Bowen's story, asking listeners to remember him, and us, in prayer.

After so much time away from the band, I needed to get on the road. Bowen's hospital bill was over half a million and running, and he had another surgery scheduled soon. We were blessed to have good insurance, but at some point you have to go back to work.

Which meant leaving Sarah alone with a sick baby and two small kids. I tried to rationalize it—the record was selling like crazy; God was providing—but the guilt was still a bear. I spent a lot of time staring out the bus window, thinking long and hard about how to find a balance between being the sole financial provider for my family while trying to step up and be the emotional and spiritual leader too.

"Lead Me" was a vulnerable message to send out into the world, but sharing my difficulties was helping a lot of other struggling people too. You'd think that hanging my dirty laundry out for the world to see would trigger my anxiety and insecurities. Strangely enough, it was the one thing that seemed to calm my restless heart. My pain had a purpose after all.

After Bowen's health crisis, I felt a burden to help other families who had children suffering from congenital heart disease, so I posted regular updates to the blog and visited children's hospitals while I was out on the road. I even started a foundation called Whole Hearts to support and assist other families.

God had been gracious to me, and I wanted to give back. I was busier than ever between family, the band, and our new charitable organization, taking no time to rest or process the trauma we'd been through. At some point of exhaustion, if you stop, you'll collapse. So I just kept running instead.

———

In February 2011, Sarah and I packed our bags and headed back to Mott Children's for Bowen's second open heart surgery, called the hemi-Fontan. The surgery fell on the same week as the fifty-third annual Grammy Awards. *Pieces of a Real Heart* had been nominated for Best Pop/Contemporary Gospel Album, so my bandmates flew to Los Angeles for the ceremonies while Sarah and I watched a live stream from our hospital room. We didn't take home a trophy that year, but I was given a better gift. Bowen's surgery went exactly as planned. Sarah and I were able to take him home after only five days.

But we were still in the whirlwind. Bowen's round-the-clock care kept Sarah overwhelmed. I was still trying to figure out how to take care of my family while keeping up with the tidal wave of demand for Sanctus Real. Sarah found herself wishing that I would spend more time at Bowen's bedside, learning about his disease. I started to feel like I was losing my companion, that our marriage was fading into an abyss of medical terms.

Sadness and isolation crept in. Sarah and I grieved differently and separately as well, which meant there was a gap where resentment began to creep in.

I loved the band and understood that music required a lot of time and sacrifice. But I was drowning at home and needed to know that Matt was making our needs his first priority. It was a tough situation on both sides. —Sarah

We couldn't see our problems with any clarity back then. We were just trying to survive one day at a time. I didn't expect Sarah to neglect Bowen, and she didn't expect me to quit my job.

Life blindsides us sometimes. Most of us feel like we're doing the best we can. Distance grows slowly. One day we wake up miles apart, not even sure how we got so far away.

———

I feel so deeply for families as they face unexpected tragedy. At some point we all go through it. Walking through loss or trials is difficult, but the tsunami of emotion that comes after the earthquake can be equally as devastating. It's more than enough to tear a family apart.

In the hospital, Sarah and I saw our fair share of parents walking out the doors alone, with empty car seats and bags of their children's belongings. Sharing tears and an embrace can bring a little comfort, but

nothing can make it better for those grieving. Words just aren't suffi-
cient. Only God knows what each heart suffers in loss. Healing is a long
road.

In my own marriage, I've found it very difficult to know how to
care for Sarah when I'm hurting too. I've learned the hard way that I
can't be the husband she needs me to be if I'm ignoring or running from
my own pain. When I've kept it all bottled up inside, I usually end up
taking it out on Sarah and the kids through streaks of impatience or
outbursts of anger.

One thing that has helped tremendously is opening up to people I
trust about what I'm feeling instead of glossing it over or sweeping it
under the rug. When a friend asks me how I'm doing, I'm finally mus-
tering up the courage to say "not well" when it's the truth. Confession
is the first step toward healing.

Think About It

1. Big dreams require big sacrifices. There's no way around that. I'm wondering, what is a big dream, or even a not-so-big dream, you're chasing right now? Let me encourage you to name a few sacrifices that have been required of you so far.

2. One of the big tensions in this section is juggling the demands of family and career. Consider your experiences with such juggling, whether personal experiences or others' experiences you've observed. Is the juggling possible? Is it inevitable that something gets dropped? Who could you point to if I asked you for a good example of a couple keeping up with all of life's demands.

3. "Without authentic community, people burn out from faking it." Do you believe that statement? Why or why not? Have you ever had such a community, where you could openly give and receive the best and the worst and all the in-between? If not, are you seeking friends who will challenge you to grow in your life and faith?

4. When a spouse or friend approaches you with a need or a concern, what is, in most cases, your first response? Are you more prone to listen or to defend

yourself/dilute his or her feelings? Again, in most cases, is this serving you and that relationship well? Why or why not?

5. Research shows overwhelming divorce rates among couples who become parents of chronically ill children. Partners often grieve differently and separately from each other, drifting further apart instead of closer together. It may or may not be a sick child, but is there some pain or loss that you're grieving? How do you and your spouse process pain differently? What efforts are you making to let your grief pull you together and not apart?

6. If you don't know the exact reference (Romans 8:28), I'm guessing you've heard a variation of the verse before—"All things work together for good, for those who are called according to his purpose." Do you really believe that? If yes, what or who can you point to that shores up that belief? If no, who or what has caused you to doubt?

Father, Show
Me the Way

35

The Dirt

'∨e had people ask me for the behind-the-scenes dirt on Sanctus Real. Well, here it is. We didn't argue enough. Maybe we should've hashed it out, hugged it out, had a few more knock-down, drag-out fights. I don't know; we just held so much inside. I always considered my band-mates to be my best friends, but for some reason we struggled to find the level of vulnerability and connection that we all desired. Our bond was thicker than blood, but our communication remained too thin. Perhaps we were more like brothers in that sense.

As a band of brothers, we soldiered on, releasing a deluxe edition of *Pieces of a Real Heart* as well as *Pieces of Our Past: The Sanctus Real Anthology,* which contained our first three records in a single collection of discs. Also, on the anniversary of Bowen's first open heart surgery, I released my first solo project, *Every Falling Tear,* a collection of those personal psalms and lullabies I'd written during the months between Bowen's diagnosis and birth. The crunchy guitars and punk-pop stylings were long gone. It was ten songs of sorrow and struggle and trying not to lose my way in the dark.

To keep Sanctus Real afloat and family finances flowing, I committed to back-to-back, forty-city arena tours. Maybe I could bulldoze through my burdens by staying busy, leaving those worries dead in the road behind me, forgetting they were there. But I've seen the movie enough times to know that you can never assume the monster is really dead before you turn your back and walk away.

Every monster has a name. It's scary to say the names out loud sometimes, because validating their existence means they might be real. This is the first time I've stated it so plainly, and it took me almost a decade to get here—but it feels good to say it by name now. I was depressed.

I worked to play it down, frame it with ten thousand words that sound better. Words like *depression* feel so rigid and clinical. They carry the weight of the darkest stories they spin.

My story wasn't so crazy; I was simply hiding my broken heart with a smile. The posttraumatic stress from my experiences in the hospital with Bowen added layers that I could point to and blame instead of looking beyond that to my cracked foundation.

I should've sought counseling, but I never did. My bandmates seemed concerned; I think they felt it. But no one knew how bad it was at the time. Not even me.

As our big fall tour got rolling, we parted ways with a manager we really loved. His loss left a void, and it was another tough blow for us all. It felt like we were in the deep end, out of breath, out of strength, out of rope. And now we had even more responsibility. We needed help, and we needed it quick.

We began our search for a new manager, knowing it would be difficult to find someone as passionate as we were about the day-to-day work of Sanctus Real. While the band needed help, I needed a friend. I felt desperate for someone to lend an ear, to offer godly counsel through the challenges I found myself up against. If I had someone to lean on besides Sarah, then maybe I wouldn't be so emotionally dependent on her. Maybe I'd find it easier to be that rock that she needed me to be.

The physical attraction between Sarah and me never faded, but every time I heard someone say that his spouse was his best friend, I felt like I was missing out on something. I watched Sarah laugh, cry, and share her deepest thoughts and feelings with her best friends. I wanted that too.

———

One day the guys were out grabbing coffee before the show, and I stayed behind, holing up in my bunk as usual, headphones on, listening to some message from John Piper about glory. In a spell of loneliness, I decided to roll out of my bunk and wander the halls of the venue, making small talk with people along the way.

I sat on a road case and struck up a conversation with a person I'd met but never really talked to before. We soon became fast friends, and it felt good to open up, to have someone listen, to feel affirmed. It became the first of many long, heartfelt conversations between us.

Lucy was older, kind, and caring. Best I could tell, she was an incredible wife and had raised wonderful children. She was a hard worker who would do anything for her friends. Lucy lived life with open hands and an open heart. I clung to that, as hurting people do.

I told Sarah the good news. "I think this could be the person we've been praying for," I said. "Not only is she an amazing friend, but I think she has what it takes to help the band." I assured her that Lucy was a total godsend and the perfect timing of it all was the evidence. Without having met Lucy, Sarah felt a little uncomfortable with how quickly our friendship was developing. Still, she supported me.

Our new manager worked overtime and found unique ways of making us all feel loved and cared for. Nicknames for everyone, little gifts in our bunks, intentional bonding moments with the band.

People like to crack jokes and belittle lead singers, as if they need to put us back in our place. Lucy never did that. She said that I was special, even asking me to take one of those personality tests so she could better understand where I was coming from. It caught me off guard but also made me feel good when she admitted that she'd been searching for someone like me too. "Matt, you're my best friend," Lucy told me late one night after a show. "And I hope that I can be yours too."

It took me a moment to answer because I had so deeply longed to hear those words from someone. "I don't really know if I'm comfortable with that," I replied sheepishly but honestly.

"God has made me a confidant for many good men," Lucy explained. "It's always been that way."

"Oh," I replied. I was probably worrying over nothing. Anxiety sends off a lot of false alarms. "Okay. Sure."

Lucy was there for me—but male or female, that's what good managers do. Support their band. Listen. Solve problems. The support felt good. Probably a little too good.

36

Message to Broken Me

The LORD is close to the brokenhearted;

he rescues those whose spirits are crushed.

—PSALM 34:18, NLT

The band hit the road for another forty-city tour. Sarah and I had fought another ruthless uncivil war before I left. The worst fights seemed to take place just as I was packing to go, and this time Sarah unloaded both barrels on me. What was I supposed to do? *Sorry, guys, I guess it'll have to be nine bands for ten bucks. Can you just charge nine for nine? What's that? You already made a hundred thousand posters?*

Heading back out on the road had always been tough, but I was hurt and frustrated enough to look forward to time apart. A bus bunk is like your own minicave. Pitch black, cold, nothing but the sound of the engine beneath you. I climbed in, pulled my curtain shut and fell into a heavy sleep.

Hours later I woke up in a panic, rolling out of bed with the realization I had only minutes to spare before sound check. I pushed the bus door open. The winter sun blinded my eyes as I grabbed my guitar case from under the bus and the handle broke as I was pulling it out.

"Oh, come ON!" I yelled, fighting the urge to throw that six-string as far as I could and walk until I hit the ocean. I took a deep breath, wrapped my arms around the case and headed backstage.

Our latest battle started replaying through my mind, Sarah's accusations echoing, stinging me again: *I'm home caring for our sick child day in and day out, and you're NEVER here.*

I practiced better responses.

What are you talking about?! I was just home for THREE straight days. What do you want from me?

Sarah's voice continued in my head. *I can't do this anymore. I feel like I am ALWAYS on my own.*

Really, Sarah? Always? I stirred myself to self-righteous indignation. *This is not a hobby; it's my job! I'm a traveling MUSICIAN. You knew this before we got married. How do you think we're going to pay these hospital bills?*

Despite the mental distractions, I made it inside and slipped up onto the stage, quiet, head down. The guys could tell when things were bad, I think. After sound check, I grabbed a cup of coffee and pulled up a chair across from Lucy. Before long, I was venting to her about my clash with Sarah. Validation, sympathy. It was all wind in my sails, and I needed it.

Lucy listened intently. "Matt, you're a good man," she said. "Sarah is *so* lucky to have someone like you."

"Yeah, I guess," I said, drinking it up, fishing for more. "It just feels like I'm doing my best, ya know?"

Showtime came, but I still couldn't shake the self-pity. We circled for prayer before heading to the stage. The band looked to me to lead so I closed my eyes and began.

"Father, we stand here humbled that we're able to serve You with our music and words. We pray that Your will be done through us and that we would look past our own agendas to accomplish Yours. We pray for those who need encouragement and for those who simply need You. Let it be not for us, but for Your glory, Lord . . ."

You ever start praying, and at first you're going through the motions, saying the familiar phrases—and then suddenly Jesus shows up for real?

It felt spiritual, but physical too. Peace like heat through my veins reaching into every part of me, wrapping me like a blanket in the cold. The prayer circle was silent, arms around shoulders, waiting. I took a deep breath.

"And Father . . . I pray for hardened hearts. For lives that need to be changed by Your truth and Your presence tonight. Break walls. Open eyes. Remove every obstacle that stands in the way of surrender. Amen."

I handed my phone to Lucy to hold during the show. The lights went down. We slipped out into the stands and waited for the cue to begin. Spotlights dotted each one of us as we stood among the audience. A sea of hands reached out around me as I started to sing.

"Take Over Me" segued into "The Face of Love." All my troubles faded as I sprinted toward the stage. There was something different about this show, the presence of God heavy, like a storm cloud in the room. Like for just one moment, time and gravity loosened their grip, and the boundary between heaven and earth fell away.

Each song took us higher, breaking us, shaping us, piecing us back together again, our arms lifted, ten thousand voices as one.

How long had we been playing? Five minutes? Five hours? It was hard to tell. I grabbed my water bottle and checked the set list. Reality crashed my spiritual high. There it was, written in bold black Sharpie, the last song of the night: LEAD ME.

I took a long sip and strummed through the intro, buying time, looking out over the arena, faces soft-lit in blue. Just when I think our career is over, a song rises up and takes us to new heights. One little, bittersweet, sad but hopeful song that reminds me how far I fall short.

Scenes from the "Lead Me" video flashed across the giant screens behind me, a lonely wife and kids. I was still angry about the stuff Sarah had said. A lot of it didn't seem fair. But then again, I'd said a lot of harsh things too.

I hated that we'd struggled so much, that I'd let her down, that life had not turned out the way we had hoped or planned. So much disappointment, so much confusion. So much anger and pain. But despite all that, I could not deny this one simple truth: I was committed through thick and thin to that woman. She was a gift from God to me.

That preshow prayer about walls being broken, eyes being opened? It was for me. I was blinded by my career, my needs, my dreams. My heart was so hard. I was the one who needed to be changed.

I crumbled under the weight of conviction. The audience took over, a thousand voices judging me by my own words. The spotlight faded, and I stood in the dark, silent, as a choir of voices sang out.

Oh, Father, show me the way to lead them
won't you lead me?

In that moment of darkness, I could see again. "Lead Me" had become Matt Hammitt's message to broken families, but it was still God's message to broken *me*.

After the concert, I was quiet while packing up my gear. Chris passed me in the front lounge of the bus. "You okay, man?" he asked.

"Feels like I'm coming down with something," I replied. "Think I'm gonna go try to sleep it off."

"Sure you don't want to spin some Heartbreakers or watch *Nacho Libre* again?" Chris and I had been friends since tenth grade. I guess he knew when I was pretending. Did he?

"Nah, man. Need to sit this one out." I headed down the hall, climbed in my bunk, and pulled the curtain shut, lying there in my stage clothes, too sapped to even pull up a blanket. I could hear everyone laughing, telling stories, and listening to music into the night. I wanted to join them, but sometimes when you're lonely, you don't want company. Yeah, yeah. I know.

Hours later I was woken by a hand reaching in to gently squeeze mine. A voice whispered in the dark, "Hey, you okay?" It was Lucy.

"Oh, hey. Yeah." I replied, cracking open the curtain to offer a smile. She smiled back and walked away.

This had become the norm between us. A gentle word, a squeeze of the hand, a lingering embrace. Throughout the day, we exchanged a constant thread of thoughtful text messages and kind words. Our texts were never scandalous, just overly emotional and friendly at times.

My anxiety flared every time a notification lit up my screen because each message represented a choice. Accept or reject. I always paused before hitting Send. Sometimes I'd delete a thread out of guilt or fear that it might get back to Sarah. If you're deleting texts from the opposite sex, that's probably a sign something isn't right.

When I brought up my concerns to Lucy, it became clear her boundaries were different from mine. Not all bad, but different.

Choosing friendship with Lucy would mean choosing to live outside my comfort zone.

I hadn't crossed any irreparable lines with Lucy, nor did I want to. But healthy boundaries and trust were being broken. The situation was reaching a tipping point, and I was spending what little energy I had left to keep it from tumbling in the wrong direction. I knew full well that something needed to change. But knowing something and changing it are two very different things.

I wasn't the only one with concerns. As Sarah began to spend more time around Lucy, there was a growing disconnect. "I figured your new best friend would show more interest in getting to know your wife," Sarah said. I defended Lucy and assured Sarah that everything was fine. But I knew better than that.

37

Home Fires Burning

When you pass through the waters, I will be with you;
and through the rivers, they shall not overwhelm you;
when you walk through fire you shall not be burned,
and the flame shall not consume you.

—ISAIAH 43:2

As time dragged on, I hoped that my depression and tangled emotions would sort themselves out. Months of back-to-back days on the road had finally come to an end, and I had some time off to get my head straight. Hopefully, my marriage too.

There's something I should reveal at this point. I can't get away with using it as a cliffhanger anymore. Maybe you can guess?

Surprise! We were pregnant!

Sarah and I agreed that our family felt incomplete, but with everything else that was going on, we didn't plan to bring another baby into the mix just yet. But how could we not be excited? Every child is a gift from God.

We knew there was a small chance of having another infant with special needs, and I worried that it wouldn't be fair to Claire and Emmy. They'd already been through so much.

Then again, they adored Bowen. It was so cute to watch them all together. Even though we had plenty of natural fears and concerns, we believed that God had big plans for our growing family, so we placed our trust in Him.

Sanctus Real was scheduled to play a one-off show at a theme park out east. I saw an opportunity for Sarah and me to get out and have some fun with the girls. Maybe it could ease some of the tension we'd been feeling. We arranged for Claire and Emmy to come along on the bus for the show. Bowen's condition had improved enough that we felt okay leaving him with his Grammy Pammy, Sarah's mom. He loved swimming in great-grandma Gloria's pool, so he would have plenty of fun.

Mark brought his boys on the trip too. It was a great adventure for the kids. After the show, we packed up our gear and spent the rest of the day with family indulging in funnel cakes and kiddie rides. As the park closed, we wrangled our sweaty, worn-out little ones back onto the bus.

Our tour bus was set up like most. Front lounge with two facing couches, a booth, and a kitchenette. Beyond that, there was a hallway lined with twelve bunks, each with private curtains. Walk past the bunks and there's a back lounge with closets, another TV, and a wraparound couch that turned into a bed. Sarah and the girls preferred to sleep back there.

Somewhere around 3 a.m., the bus engine cut out. No drone, no hum. Silence. Sarah sat up. She heard the bus tires buzzing over the rumble strip as our driver, Steph, pulled to the side of the road. Suddenly, there was an explosion behind the engine wall, only a few feet from where Emmy and Claire lay sound asleep. The blast shot flames up the side of the rear window, leaving the back lounge flooded with smoke and the smell of burning wires.

"Get her and run!" Sarah shouted, pushing Claire to me as I rolled out groggy from my bunk. Sarah headed back, yelling for Emmy. But Emmy is a hard sleeper and would not get up.

Sarah was four months pregnant. Emmy was too tall to carry. "Get up, Emmy! Get up!" she screamed as fire cracked the glass.

I muscled Emmy down the hall as everyone scrambled to get out. It was pure adrenaline. I was expecting another explosion at any second. —Sarah

We stood half-dressed on the Pennsylvania Turnpike, watching the flames leap higher. "Run!" cried Sarah. "Get as far away as you can!"

Everybody ran farther back. Steph kept running, all the way to the mile marker so she could call 911 and tell them where we were. Tires popped, hissing out air. Windows shattered in the heat. State Troopers had to stop traffic both ways, and it still took the fire trucks twenty minutes to arrive.

There were no hydrants so the firefighters ran out of water several times. One firefighter fell off a ladder into the back lounge and broke his wrist. Laptops, wallets, cell phones, clothes. We didn't have time to save anything. All we could do was watch it burn.

The sun broke over Blue Mountain as they sprayed down the last ashes. Our bus was a smoldering shell. I embraced Sarah and the girls, pushing my nose into their hair, breathing in the scent of home. Physically, we were unscathed, but it wasn't easy on our hearts.

It was the first time I felt mad at God. Like, really? Everything with Bowen and now this? There was an explosion next to my sleeping children? I almost lost my *healthy* kids? I wrestled with God so much during that time. —Sarah

It was a kick in the face when we were already down, but I believe it's best to try to learn something from our trials. Stuff is just stuff. That's what the bus fire showed me. Don't get attached to the things that can be burned, stolen, or destroyed by rust.

Our insurance policy wasn't enough to even cover what was lost, much less to buy a new bus. Fans and fellow artists sent in donations. Some even offered use of their tour buses so we could carry on. The cost was crippling, but it was good to know we had friends who loved and cared for us.

Standing on the side of that highway, watching my home away from home go up in flames was hard. It had already been a long season of hard lessons and loss. But my wife and kids were safe in my arms.

———

Watching our bus burn was a wake-up call. In some weird way, it felt like a metaphor, a warning to me about what could happen to my marriage and family if I didn't make some clear and hard choices. I'd watched one home go up in flames—would it be two? I couldn't let that happen. I already knew that something needed to change, but here I was standing in that same familiar place. Was I going to take my good intentions and turn them into actions? Would I protect and preserve what God had given me to care for?

Shifting boundaries and emotional confusion had me in a deadly pattern with Lucy. But it was more than that. We had made her the ambassador of our business, the guardian of our privacy, given her all the passwords. She was entangled in every aspect of my life. This would be no easy break.

I picked up the phone and dialed Lucy. "Hey. Sorry, I, um . . . You got a minute?"

"For you, always. What's up?"

I fumbled into the most tongue-tied apology possible. I rambled, praying the words were coming out in the appropriate way. But there is no appropriate way other than, "There are so many things I am grateful to you for . . . but I'm just uncomfortable with how things have become between us."

There was a tense silence. Finally, Lucy spoke. "Wow, okay," she said. "Huh. I don't really know what to say."

The disappointment in her voice speared me. I remembered the things she'd said to me about loyalty and rules of friendship that were so important to her. She had warned me that I would turn out like the others who had abandoned her. I didn't want to let Lucy down.

"I guess this means I won't see you again," she said.

"What?" I replied, confused as the weight of her words began to sink in. I had been so naive. What other direction could this be taking?

"Okay, see you . . . ," Lucy lingered, but I tossed out a quick and anxious goodbye.

I once heard a therapist say that progress is a series of small epiphanies, tiny breakthroughs, the determination to keep trying, keep talking, knowing that people are messy but love is worth the fight. At some point, change is what you wake up and do differently. It's prayers for help with the things we cannot change. It's accepting that without God's help, you can't even change yourself, much less anyone else.

Now and then we get the instant miracle, but usually change takes a long process of trial and error and hard work. That's usually how God teaches us, through the process and the work. I'd love to tell you that our marriage turned around just as quickly as the actors in the "Lead Me" video, that by the end of the song, the husband had come home humble and everything was happy and fixed. But Sarah and I had hurt each other deeply, so progress was slow. A few steps forward, a few back. We did our best to connect with the time we had and rebuild our intimacy.

Every time I'm at the home of my friends Jake and Linsey, I'm drawn to a small paper clipping that hangs on their fridge. It's a copy of their wedding vows.

Jake's promises: *I commit my whole self to you. No other woman will have any part of me.* Linsey's vows, *I take you, Jacob, to be my husband and best friend. I commit my whole self to you. No other man on this earth will have any part of me, neither emotionally nor physically.*

Sarah and I had failed to find that kind of intimate friendship with each other. Instead of seeking to be that for her, I made the mistake of looking elsewhere.

I'm not claiming that married folks can't have friends of the opposite sex, and this isn't a conversation about jealousy. It's about using wisdom to prioritize those you love the most by creating boundaries that can save you from experiencing the pain and consequences of unfaithfulness in all its forms.

Before I met Lucy, I had never been in a position to consider the full scope of faithfulness in marriage. It never occurred to me that I was susceptible in any form. Now I can see that my friendship with Lucy had put a pinhole in the lining of my marriage. The emotional intimacy that belonged to Sarah had been slowly leaking out and draining the well of cherishing love that belonged only to her.

Unfaithfulness is not just romance, pornography, or sex. Those acts are obvious and often hold the greatest consequences. But sometimes even paths that look like a blessing can lead you to the gates of hell.

———

My relationship with Lucy didn't end as simply as a phone call. In fact, it was something of a disaster. But those details aren't necessary here.

I had hurt Sarah, and that's what mattered most. It wasn't the too-close friendship or even my codependence. Sarah could have dealt with all that. It was the fact that I had lied, promising everything was all right when I knew it was wrong. I didn't trust her intuition, so I spent what little I had left to give trying to protect myself instead.

I discovered it wouldn't be one conversation, but a long process of understanding and winning back trust. I started by learning to listen, not only to Sarah's words but also to her heart. I practiced validating her feelings and not just blankly nodding or thinking about what I wanted to say next. I prayed, *Lord, give me wisdom,* a thousand times. Most of all, I sought her forgiveness, while not expecting her to forget.

The collision of repentance and grace gave birth to a new depth that Sarah and I had longed for in our relationship. Most of all, I found that best friend I'd been looking for. She had been right beside me all along.

Hope deferred makes the heart sick,
but a longing fulfilled is a tree of life. (Proverbs 13:12, NIV)

———

Emmy and Claire were upset about losing their special blankies in the fire, and we were all feeling scorched by posttraumatic stress. But for the most part, the Hammitt family bounced back. Bowen was going down the big slide at the playground, and seeing him standing up there so tall and fearless in his Superman shirt filled my heart with hope for better days. I was trading ashes for beauty, mourning for gladness, and despair for praise.

The doctors at U of M did a heart cath on Bowen and told us that his heart was as strong as it could be for a child with HLHS. Sarah had her twenty-week ultrasound, and once again we sat in that dark room at the OB/GYN office, watching the mystery of life unfold on a fuzzy black and white screen.

"Congratulations," the doctor told us. "Far as I can tell, you've got a healthy baby boy in there."

———

You will know the truth, and the truth will set you free.
(John 8:32, NIV)

All the signs suggested that life was about to turn a new leaf, but it hadn't turned just yet. There was healing that needed to happen in me if I was going to lead my family well. But the thought of being at all concerned with my own health or feelings at that time felt deeply selfish, and quite honestly, pathetic. I wanted to pull myself together and be strong, but instead I experienced a kind of sadness I had never known. The spiritual vultures were circling overhead.

All of us have voices that whisper to us and the words they say are rarely good. Most people hear things like "You're going to fail," "You're not enough," or "You don't have what it takes." They're subtle, they're pesky, and they're consistent.
—Al Andrews

The vultures were the voices, and they were slowly eating away at me. I didn't recognize the man I had become. "What happened to me?" I cried out to God on a cold night. I filled the heavens with prayers for God to let me experience the joy and passion that I had once known. How had I come to such a dark place? Under my burdens, God was there, waiting for me to depend solely on Him in my brokenness.

If you've seen the movie *Captain Phillips,* you'll remember the closing scene. Tom Hanks gives a heart-wrenching performance as his character is rescued from being held hostage at sea. It was hard for me to keep it together as I watched him sob uncontrollably, lost in the truth that he had been found. And the words spoken to him, "You're safe now," are so powerfully simple in that moment.

That's what it was like for me as I reached the end of myself. I let go of all that had been bottled up inside me for years. Gasping for breath through tears, I released my burdens and my life back to God. Reaching up from the dark night of my soul, I started to see the sun rise again. It was my "You're safe now" moment with God.

The tenderness of those wounds served as fertile ground for a type of growth that Sarah and I needed to experience in our marriage. Through complicated and clumsy conversations, along with radical honesty and grace, we began falling into a new rhythm of maturing love.

38

Run

You can run, but you can't escape what you carry with you deep down in your soul. The construction (or deconstruction) of a life leaves rubble in the heart. Sure, you can ignore it for a while. But at some point, if you want the space to live freely, you'll have to do the difficult job of cleaning it up, piece by piece. Even then you'll miss a nail or two—until you step on it later.

Sarah was still hurting in the aftermath of our Lucy saga, and I was trying hard to win back her trust. I didn't always do it right, but I was committed to learning. Husbands can be prone to telling their wives snippets of truth to keep peace. Why rock the boat unnecessarily? In this case, Sarah wanted to know every miniscule detail—so that's what I gave her, spilling it all out with a surplus of words.

I know it wasn't right to look for affirmation from another woman, but it comforted me. Yes, I deleted texts. No, they weren't romantic or explicit. I wish I could say the flattery didn't feel good, but it did. Was it an affair? That word seems to suggest a lot of things that didn't happen. Still, that's no excuse. I took pieces of myself that were meant only for you and shared them with someone else. Sarah, I'm just so, *so* sorry.

Having a baby on the way drew Sarah and me closer, but the bond was precarious. At any moment, a song or a scene on TV could trigger hurt feelings, and we'd find ourselves clashing and having to start all over again. I'd made a mess of things, and it was my job to sit still, listen, and let Sarah process her pain as many times as needed.

————

Sanctus Real remained in a bind. I know it seems relentless. It was. No management, no help on the road, hustling to organize dates and keep the machine rolling. *Pieces of a Real Heart* had sold several hundred thousand copies, making it our most successful record to date. Sparrow was pressuring us hard for a follow-up.

Our long-time producer, Chris Stevens, was working overtime with TobyMac, so we enlisted Seth Mosley and Jason Ingram to help finish the album.

How many records had I made while tracking Sarah's trimesters? Four in a row. That's how many. Because what would a new Sanctus Real record be without a new Hammitt baby? Goodness. I felt a little like Bill Murray in *Groundhog Day.*

I was halfway across the desert when Sarah went into labor with Emmy, scrambling to catch a flight, barely arriving home in time for my first baby's birth. Claire had a meningitis scare while I was stuck in England. And then Bowen's heart. I was bracing myself for Lewis's arrival, wondering what unexpected tribulations might accompany baby number four. Sarah was the one who typically worried the most about our children, but she had a peace that I hadn't seen for some time. It was refreshing to my spirit.

Sarah's intuition was spot on. We went to the hospital. Lewis was born. The doctor smiled and handed him over. We brought our new baby home.

I parked in the drive and reached for the baby carrier. Sarah and I exchanged looks. No tubes. No crisis. No meds. No army of doctors. No complications. "Could having a baby really be this simple?" I said. We erupted with giddy laughter. We made it! In so many more ways than one.

In the midst of all our surrounding storms, the birth of Lewis Will-Edmond Hammitt was a much-needed moment of peace. He was calm and cool, no worries. Until he wanted milk, that is. Then he would let out a series of snorts that could call hogs in from the field.

We named him Lewis after my grandfather. Will, after Sarah's dad William, whose father died when he was young.

And Edmond? For my Grandpa Hammitt, whose life and stories filled my heart with wonder.

Edmond Hammitt was born in Brooklyn in 1924. His father abandoned the family, leaving his mother too poor to care for her children alone. They were temporarily placed in the state's care, but after their mother died, Edmond and his brother, Ray, were separated and raised as orphans in the Bronx.

Young Edmond was eyewitness to the Hindenburg disaster, watching as men in suits and women in fancy dresses leaped to their deaths. He was a gunman in World War II, shooting kamikazes down. They were so close, he said, that he could see the whites of their eyes as they raced toward his battleship. As an artist, Eddie drew sketches from the war that now grace the walls of the Eisenhower Presidential Library and Museum in Kansas. My favorite story is from his days in the orphanage.

Grandpa told us that when he wasn't sneaking out to dismantle the head mother's spanking machine (!!!), he would sit at the back of the orphanage yard, dangling his feet over the wall, looking down at the railroad tracks that ran below.

That lonesome whistle would blow, and the ground rumbled as the train approached. *Thump, thump. Thump, thump.* One day, Eddie heard a different message coming down the line. This time the wheels called to him as they passed. *Jump, jump. Jump, jump.*

Edmond Hammitt took his first free fall into an empty coal car, the first of countless rides down the railroad tracks of the Northeast United States. He became a train hopper, always running, always searching for that place called *home*.

Something about my grandfather's train hopping resonates in my soul. It's the story of every heart, isn't it? Aching, longing, searching to find your place. I have felt this way in life more times than I care to admit. Yes, even after I met the Lord.

Lewis Will-Edmond was born into the same world his great-grandpa Eddie and I inhabited, and he wouldn't be immune to the restlessness that muddies our souls. But I knew one thing for sure. I wanted to be the kind of father who was present, heart and hands, to make sure he and all my children always knew their way home.

39

Starting Over

It was a historic home, built in 1923, with high ceilings, original wood floors, built-in china cabinets in the dining room, and crown molding throughout. It had all the charm we wanted and required just enough work to make it affordable for us.

The interior of our new home was in pretty good shape, but our backyard was a twisted mass of vines snaking from untrimmed trees, weeds growing wild at every corner. There was a path of broken bricks leading to the house that would flood with the slightest rain. The remains of a limestone patio lay buried in dead, yellow grass.

If there was any potential, I wasn't able to see it. Until our neighbor told me that the previous owner was a skilled gardener and our backyard had once been the most beautiful on the block. "Mrs. Wolf kept this yard immaculate," the neighbor said, gazing at my weeds as if they were magnificent. "Beds of roses, long rows of tulips, purple garden phlox scattered with yarrow and sage. On warm days, the ladies of the neighborhood would gather here for afternoon tea."

Sadly, Mrs. Wolf was diagnosed with Alzheimer's and could no longer care for her garden. Nature took over again. Ugliness thrived and beauty died. "Such a shame," our neighbor said, shaking her head. "It breaks my heart to see it this way."

I stood with Sarah after the neighbor left, staring at this *Jurassic Park* jungle that was now our own. "What should we do?" Sarah asked.

"Buy some wild monkeys?" I replied. Sarah laughed, but we both knew we had to make something beautiful of those gardens again.

I got out there bright and early the next morning, work gloves on, shovel in hand. What a giant mess. I didn't even know where to start.

I thought about that big backyard that God gave Adam and Eve. It was perfect and lush, and in it Adam and Eve had a life of pure creativity, their sole purpose to enjoy God and His creation. It was heaven on earth. But this is life after the Fall, and now I've got a garden full of weeds. Thousands of years later, we are still feeling that curse.

I waded into the wilderness, pulling down vines, hacking dandelions, attacking thick patches of clover. *Wait. That is clover, right? How many leaves does poison ivy have?*

An hour later, I was itchy, frustrated, and soaked with sweat. I leaned against the weathered wood fence and wiped my forehead. My yard didn't look one bit different than it did before. I was in way over my head. I needed help. And I knew exactly who to call.

———

A friend had introduced me to Kraig a few months earlier. He was a jack-of-all-trades construction guy with all the tools and know-how to build or remodel just about anything you could imagine. Kraig had an army of backhoes, skid loaders, and machines I'd never heard of, let alone be able to operate.

Kraig drove over in his one-ton diesel pickup, stepped out, and greeted me with a smile and his outstretched oil-stained hand. "Yeah,

Matt, this might take more than gloves and a shovel," he said, surveying my situation. "I'd say keep the shade trees but everything else has got to go."

With Kraig's help, I gutted that yard and started over, transforming our jungle back into a space that friends and family could enjoy. After the ground was cleared, that clean slate looked so enormous that our vision continued to expand. Soon, Sarah and I were looking over plans for a music studio, right outside our back door. What had once been a creative space for Mrs. Wolf would become a place of creativity for me too.

As we stood there looking over our land, it struck me that this backyard was a lot like my marriage. The potential was there, but it took a huge effort just to get to ground zero. I couldn't build on top of years of bad growth. First, I had to clean up.

In the beginning, life and marriage were beautiful by design. Adam and Eve had it all. It's staggering to realize that out of 1,189 chapters in the Bible, there are only two before the first couple mess it up. *Two* short chapters. But is it really any surprise?

I'm drawn to a few simple yet powerful words from this story of the Fall in Genesis, chapter 3. He *was with her* in the garden. "She took of its fruit and ate, and she also gave some to her husband who was with her, and he ate" (verse 6).

What was Adam doing as Eve bit into that forbidden piece of fruit? He was with her. Why didn't he speak up? Was he distracted? Afraid to upset Eve by stepping in? Did he keep his mouth shut because he was hoping to get lucky that night? I have another theory and nothing to support it but my own mischievous heart. Let's just say it wouldn't surprise me if Adam was thinking, *I've always wanted to see if God was bluffing. I'll let her take the fall to find out.*

I can't help but wonder how the world might be different if Adam hadn't been so passive that day. If he had protected and preserved what God had given him to care for, instead of joining his wife for a taste of innocence lost.

The first couple traded innocence for shame, joyful communion to heap blame on each other. They were divided and exposed, both physically and spiritually. Their first instinct was to hide from God, afraid to be seen as they really were.

"Who told you that you were naked?" God asked. He already knew.

Instead of accepting responsibility, they pointed the finger. "It was Eve's fault!" Adam replied. "She gave me the fruit and I ate it."

"The serpent deceived me," Eve said, passing the blame on. "He told me the fruit was good, so I ate it."

With a heavy heart, God banished His most precious creatures from the garden forever. Under the curse, Adam would chase his work in the field, while Eve would chase after Adam's heart.

And here we are now, looking back on the ideal world of Eden, looking ahead to a new heaven and earth. Between the glorious beginning and eternal end is the here and now, where the curse remains a harsh reality of the human experience. We share our joy and pain, wrestling with self and others, the losses and victories common to us all.

We know Adam and Eve's story so well that it's tempting to think of it as ancient history, irrelevant to modern times. But there it was, mine and Sarah's story too, from the very beginning, over six thousand years ago. A woman longing for intimacy and a man distracted by work.

We all have a garden to tend. The garden of life and marriage isn't so different from that literal garden bed outside the doors of our homes.

So often I see landscaping overgrown by weeds, kind of like my own backyard before it was restored. I can't tell what plants or flowers are supposed to be there or even if there ever were flowers.

Who's responsible for that? I think to myself. *Where is the gardener?* The garden of love and marriage demands this same question. The answer? The gardener is me. The gardener is you.

There's a simple truth that makes this job of relational gardening especially difficult. And it's something that won't change for now. *In the face of neglect, what's beautiful dies and what's ugly thrives.* What I'd give for it to be the other way around. For flowers to bloom with no care, for weeds to die without a fight.

Taking up responsibility and facing this truth has driven me to ask another set of questions about my garden. *What needs to go, and what needs to grow?* The answer defines the job that lies ahead of me. As the gardener, I have a choice. I can be mindful of the weeds in my garden as they grow and gently pluck them at the root. Or I can let those weeds grow up tall, only to spend countless hours and amounts of energy fighting to pull them from the ground, hoping to restore the beauty that's been overtaken while I neglected the problem.

Just as it is in tending a real garden, meeting Sarah's and the kids' needs isn't something I can do only once. I have to tend them daily with perseverance, love, and devotion. I often ask myself, *What do I want the garden of my marriage and family to look like in a year, ten years, fifty years from now?* If I want it to be healthy and thriving, I need to take time to gently pluck the weeds that are growing up in it today, keeping them from taking deep root and suffocating the legacy I want to leave for generations to come.

40

It Was Time

I will boast all the more gladly about my weaknesses,
so that Christ's power may rest on me. That is why,
for Christ's sake, I delight in weaknesses, in insults, in
hardships, in persecutions, in difficulties. For when I
am weak, then I am strong.

—2 CORINTHIANS 12:9-10, NIV

In just one moment, your whole perspective can change. I wanted to help others, to minister and serve. But what is ministry at the expense of those you love?

Maybe some people can balance the road life and family, but I never could seem to make it work. Could I have made it as a successful front man if I was distracted or rarely showing up for our concerts? How could I expect to be a good husband and father if I didn't show up at home?

I had good intentions. But intentions are worthless until they become actions. Authenticity is who we are, not the person we want or pretend to be.

Why do I do the things that I hate? I want to do better, but I just can't seem to get there. I am full of myself and cannot be trusted. I know the Word but still can't keep it. Sin sabotages my best intentions and gets me every time. Who will rescue me from this body of death?

If Paul wasn't ashamed to own up to his failures, then I shouldn't be either. "By grace you have been saved through faith. And this is not your own doing; it is the gift of God, not a result of works, so that no one may boast" (Ephesians 2:8–9).

Conflict is a part of life. But God works through conflict. It bends us and breaks us, forcing us from our comfort zones, making us do the hard work of getting along. I knew that it was my responsibility to be present, loving, creative, and disciplined in my relationship with Sarah and each of my kids. Most importantly, I had a responsibility to grow in my faith and relationship with God.

At 2 a.m., in the top bunk of a Prevost coach somewhere out on I-95, God began to speak to my heart. And there was no misunderstanding. This time, He was calling me to something truly new. Right then, I knew.

It was time to quit the band.

41

Farewell

I've been traveling far and wide singing the song "Lead Me," but now I want to sing it less and live it more.

—MY MESSAGE TO OUR FRIENDS, FAMILY, AND FANS

PRESS RELEASE:

Nashville, Tenn. (July 1, 2015) Sanctus Real will unveil *Best of Sanctus Real*, their last project with lead singer Matt Hammitt, on October 9, 2015. Featuring 14 of the band's top hits over their 20-year career, the compilation also includes the newly released single "Longer Than a Lifetime." In conjunction with their *Best of Sanctus Real* release, the band will embark on a Farewell to a Friend tour this fall, kicking off October 7 in Iowa Falls, Iowa.

Farewell to a friend = me.

We booked fifteen final shows to say goodbye. Iowa to Louisiana to North Carolina. And one unforgettable night in Ohio, just like we'd wished for.

I stood onstage at our sold-out homecoming show in Perrysburg. I'd never seen so many eyes intently watching me all at once. My voice cracked as I sang about a simpler time and place, back when I was sixteen, writing "Coffee of Life" for Sanctus Real. Now I was twenty years older, alone in a purple spotlight, just me and my guitar, stripping away the punk to play it slower and more contemplative instead.

The band hovered in the shadows behind me. *I'll take you somewhere you held no regrets* . . . That last lyric line echoed through the auditorium before Mark stepped up to take the mic. Some kids from Vineyard Church down the street, where Mark had just taken the position as youth pastor, started chanting his name. It warmed my heart to know he was finding his place through all this change too.

"It's kinda like that kid who gave Jesus his bit of lunch," Mark said. "We were just a bunch of kids goofing around in a basement, but we offered what little bit we had."

Mark fought back tears as he talked about the thousands of hungry people who were filled from one simple act of surrender. He talked about the years of hard work and sacrifice, the willingness to wear our hearts on our sleeve. Family members and friends who had seen our first performance at Jim's studio were there that night. It was humbling that so many still cared and wanted to celebrate what God had done over the years. Here we were, all grown up, back in Ohio. In some ways different and in another way a lot the same.

Chris took the microphone next, not one to speak much in public back then. Not a week had passed in two decades that we hadn't played music together. He told me he loved me, that he was proud, that we would continue to support one another and be friends. I fingerpicked those simple chords, head down. "Coffee of Life" isn't really a tearjerker, but there were too many to count that night.

Chris and I hugged. Everybody clapped. It felt weird to be so vulnerable under the spotlight. "Okay, so, um . . . now we're gonna rock out together some more," I said nervously, trying to change the tone. We closed the night by doing what Sanctus Real did best—pouring our hearts into every note, even the bad ones. We gave people space and permission to get lost and helped them remember how to be found. We hugged necks and signed posters, packed up our gear, and boarded the bus to Somewhereville, USA.

————

I had to detach. If I would've let myself feel everything I wanted to feel, it would have been too difficult to walk away. As much as I had grown weary of the road, the reality of the end left me unnerved. I don't know what I thought, maybe that we'd be old men shuffling through "Say It Loud" one day.

I was hoping the tour would bring emotional closure, but in truth the burden of getting the band out of debt overshadowed that hope. Sanctus Real wasn't broke, just saddled with the usual business expenses that mount up over time.

I felt an obligation to leave my bandmates in the best shape possible to carry on. So many miles and trials and tribulations shared over the years. Love looks like a thousand little things you never realize until you're saying goodbye.

I watched the miles pass outside our bus window, wondering how I was going to support my family once the tour was done. I worried about my bandmates as well, how they would provide for their loved ones. At times my heart wrenched from fear that my brothers would be ruined. I heard the Lord whisper, *Do you think you're the only child I love?* In that moment I realized how pompous it was to think that God would take care of me while neglecting His other children. My heart was humbled, put to rest. It wasn't my burden to carry any longer.

When Peter answered the call of Jesus and walked on water, I bet dipping his toe into the sea was easy compared with what came next. Imagine Peter placing the full weight of his body onto the waves, lifting his other sandal, both feet fully overboard. I bet he was terrified. Every step was a miracle. It wasn't until he took his eyes off Jesus, overwhelmed by the chaos of the storm swirling around him, that he started to fall.

Keep my heart, my eyes on You, Lord, I prayed.

I reread those stories about Peter and the disciples and took them deeply to heart. I could see how frail they were as men, trying to be strong like Jesus. I combed my way through pages of Scripture, all the way back to Adam again. Failures, doubts, insecurities. Humanity has pierced us all. But when our sins pierced Jesus, we finally saw the thread that truly connects us and mends us eternally. The apostle Paul, in his letter to the Colossians, wrote something beautiful about this truth.

We look at this Son and see the God who cannot be seen.
We look at this Son and see God's original purpose in everything created. For everything, absolutely everything, above
and below, visible and invisible, rank after rank after rank of
angels—everything got started in him and finds its purpose
in him. (Colossians 1:15–16, MSG)

Everything finds its purpose in Him. Born to share our struggles, Jesus, Son of God, shows us the way to humbly lead and lovingly sacrifice. In following Him we find our way to being as we were meant to be from the beginning. But it's so much more than simply following Jesus. It's mind blowing actually, that the voice that calls us, the hand that catches us, is the very One who holds all things together. There is a master plan, a masterpiece, and you hold a place in the mosaic of eternity, whether or not you follow the call. He has made no mistake.

But as for me, I was determined to follow. I had read the books, said all the prayers, and I meant them. Now it was time to take the other foot out of the boat and walk as Peter did toward the One who was calling me. I would learn to trust, each step of the way.

There's a seat on every tour bus that I love, shotgun to the driver, where a view of the road and the wild blue glide past you through a wall of glass. Like Leo, arms stretched wide in that scene from *Titanic*, I saw an ocean of possibilities through that windshield. I dreamed about the future and how seasons change. I felt the courage to embrace what was next and the grace to let go of what was behind.

> I do not consider that I have made it my own. But one thing I
> do: forgetting what lies behind and straining forward to what
> lies ahead. (Philippians 3:13)

On those long drives, I gained clarity about the next steps that I was meant to take. Those years of struggle had equipped me with a valuable gift. My ability to communicate about life and truth had been refined after twenty years onstage. It was time to unpack the heart of the messages I'd been whittling down into four-minute songs.

Not a day passed that I didn't hear stories of how songs like "Lead Me" had deeply impacted people from all walks of life. There was no telling how many were starving to find hope for their lives, marriages, and families. The nudge in my spirit was undeniable. I needed to take the lessons I had learned along the way and share them with others as I continued to grow.

Hammitt Family Adventures

Direction—not intention—determines your destination.

—ANDY STANLEY

When I felt sentimental about the band, time moved too fast. When I thought about spending more time with my family, it couldn't move fast enough. Before I knew it, the final Sanctus Real show had come and gone.

A friend invited me to do a short run of Christmas shows up in the Northeast. I had also been invited to speak on marriage and manhood at some events along the way. I was starting over, and it was scary and exciting all at once. I hadn't taken anything from the band, so I needed some new gear and a new way to get around. Even though my schedule was sparse in comparison to my time with Sanctus Real, I vowed to be with family. I wanted them with me, even on the road. So we did what any smart family does and bought an RV. Ever seen that Robin Williams movie, *RV*? *(clears throat)*

We went shopping for a new rig with the kids. They would run and climb through each model, screaming, "Dad, look at this! A fake fire-place! A shower!" Everything commonplace seems epic on wheels. Each model was the perfect one while my kids were in it. Plopping down on each bed, they would let out heavenly sighs. *Ahhhhh.* We finally decided on a forty-foot Thor Challenger, a full-on house on wheels.

From church to church, we rambled across the Northeast on our own Griswold family adventure, reconnecting, making up for lost time. Bowen was healthy enough to help with the show. Lewis pitched in too, while Emmy and Claire joined me onstage for a song or two. Sarah even helped work the merchandise table, just like the old days.

Our communication came back to life in that Challenger. Sarah and I went to a deeper level, the sort of connection that takes place when you're living together in tight quarters. Things were beginning to click in a way they never had before. For years Sarah had been saying, "Matt, I need you *here.*"—and that's where I was. No matter where "here" happened to be.

In the past, it felt like Matt was on the outside of our family cir-cle, and we were trying to pull him in. Now, he was the link that was connecting us, pulling us together on our first adventure as a family of six. —Sarah

God continued to impress upon me the importance of being inten-tional, not just floating around and waiting for change. Things between Sarah and me were better, but I didn't want to stop there. I wanted the best marriage possible.

Being out on a journey together proved to be the best therapy for us. Sarah and I read books on relationships, we discussed the issues we'd been sidestepping or fighting about for years, and we finally took the time to build a true friendship. The writings of Dr. Henry Cloud were especially helpful to me during this time as he spoke of living with "the courage to meet the demands of reality."

For me, the biggest change was that Matt was learning to hear my heart and accept what I was saying without trying to change or fix me. We were able to face disagreements without letting things turn toxic. —Sarah

———

"Five under, Matt," Sarah reminded me again, placing her hand on my shoulder.

That was her thing, that I should drive five miles per hour below the speed limit at all times. Sarah was the Thor's own onboard governor, sounding off a warning each time my speedometer crept toward the posted limit.

For the last two hundred miles she'd been perched just over my shoulder, offering me driving tips. First couple of hours, no big deal. Love is patient.

"Matt, watch out for the edge of the road."

"I hate big trucks. Let that guy pass."

"What's that orange light on the dash? Is that supposed to be on?"

"You're swaying, Matthew. Can you slow down a little more?"

As we drove through Pennsylvania, we passed the place where we had once stood on the side of the turnpike in our jammies while watching our bus burn down. I said a prayer of gratitude and thanked God that our family made it home. I could've lost them. So many times, in so many ways. But we were there, together, and that's what mattered most.

I crossed the New York state line with a smile, doing 53 in a 55. Or maybe it was 63. "Five under," Governor Sarah said, poking me with her finger for the umpteenth time. "Five under."

"Honey?" I replied softly, easing off the gas. *A gentle answer makes anger disappear, but a sharp tongue kindles fire.*

"Yeah, babe?" Sarah said.

"You've been clocking my miles per hour, but I've been clocking your comments per hour. And I know darn well who's going faster!"

For a split second, my heart sank. I didn't hear her laugh. *Oh no, I've started an argument,* I thought, eyes on the road. When I worked up the nerve to look over, she was smiling. *Thank God.*

We talked about the little things in marriage, those tiny triggers that set off nuclear bombs. We laughed about how many small, insignificant differences had plagued us over the years and how easily those repressed issues can be unearthed with one wrong word. Sometimes even a look.

Sarah and I now had the space to process things with respect and the goal of understanding rather than defense and counterattack. We weren't simmering in avoidance for the two days I was home and then erupting as it was time for me to leave. Our relationship was growing, and my heart was at peace.

———

My son, be attentive to my words;
    incline your ear to my sayings. . . .
Let your eyes look directly forward,
    and your gaze be straight before you.
Ponder the path of your feet;
    then all your ways will be sure.

Do not swerve to the right or to the left;

turn your foot away from evil. (Proverbs 4:20, 25–27)

Good drivers pay attention to signs that are meant to help them understand the condition of the road they are on and to help avoid dangerous or fatal situations. God has given us signs, too, to help us avoid danger on the roadway of life and relationships. Hands on the wheel, foot on the pedal, we have a say in how much damage we cause on the way to our destination.

I want to share a few signs that I didn't know how to read for a good part of my marriage. I still don't follow them perfectly, but I've found some helpful—and I believe biblical—ways to respond.

When I see a sign of anger, I want to give anger in return. But love is telling me to stay calm, be patient, and hear what my spouse is saying instead of how she is saying it.

When I see the signs of defensiveness, I want to be defensive too. But peace is whispering that something about me is making others afraid, and I need to create a safer environment.

When the signs are telling me that I'm headed in the wrong direction, I want to believe it is actually the sign that is mistaken. But wisdom is telling me to heed the warning, slow down, and find a better way.

Love allows us to stay calm, read the signs, and safely navigate the path before us. Fear on the other hand, causes confusion and chaos that can send us in the wrong direction, maybe even off the cliff. Marriage calls us down some dangerous roads where, ultimately, we have to let Jesus take the wheel. Yes, I just quoted a country song. Life is a long drive. Don't judge me for what's on the radio.

43

Wait and See

Church leaders continued to reach out, inviting me to speak at marriage and men's events. Many of them had heard the podcast that Sarah and I launched as I announced my transition out of Sanctus Real. We named it the *Lead Me Lifecast,* and over twenty-five thousand people listened to our first episode, "About My Decision to Leave Sanctus Real."

Bob Lepine from FamilyLife ministries in Little Rock also caught the show and called me up. Even as a child, I remember hearing *FamilyLife Today* on the radio in mom's car. I knew Bob's voice so well that he felt like an old friend.

"Matt, I don't know what you're up to in this new season. Might sound crazy, but how would you feel about joining our speaker team for the Weekend to Remember marriage retreats?" Bob asked.

It didn't sound crazy at all. Sarah and I had attended a FamilyLife's Weekend to Remember retreat in 2009, shortly after I'd written "Lead Me." Though things didn't change overnight, we were able to point back to the lessons and truths learned there that helped us through our most difficult times. It was an honor to think I could make the same impact on other people's lives, so I agreed to join the FamilyLife team.

———————

I was excited about new speaking opportunities but still had songs stirring in my heart and mind. My friend Seth Mosley had been inviting me to write with some artists he was producing. In June of 2016, Seth invited me to formally partner with his company, Full Circle Music, as a songwriter.

The Christian industry was still centered in Nashville, so we took a leap of faith, renting out our house in Ohio and docking the RV in Music City. We parked out past the airport at the peninsula of Percy Priest Lake, right on the beach at Safe Harbor. My music-business buddy Josh lived nearby and let me use an empty room at his studio so I could have a quiet place to write.

I was back working in music during the week and home at night for lakeside cookouts with my kids. On the weekends, we would fire up the Challenger and head out on the open road.

Campgrounds, parking lots, truck stops, freeways, and switchbacks through the mountains—the Great Hammitt Family Adventure continued. We headed to Colorado, then on to Arizona for another "Lead Me Live" event.

Sarah and I saw the perfect opportunity for a detour. We would take the kids to see the Grand Canyon for the first time. At first, they didn't get what all the fuss was about. "Da-ad!" Emmy whined. "Why are we driving so far out of our way just to see some hole in the ground?"

"It's a little more than a hole," I explained. "Just wait. You'll see."

Hours later, we steered the Challenger into a parking lot near the canyon's South Rim. We were losing sunlight fast. "Quick, guys, c'mon!" I yelled. Our jog was interrupted by a family of elk.

We tiptoed through those towering creatures, eyes the size of pool balls staring at our every move. Through the elk, down the path, around the statue, and past the visitor center just in time to see a glorious Arizona sunset. Purple, pink, orange, and yellow swept in lines to paint the sky. Rays of light beat down over jagged rock, creating an ever-evolving tapestry of shapes, colors, and dimensions that the kids had never seen.

We were speechless, in awe of the width and depth of that stunning collage. I looked at Emmy, who had wondered why we drove so far to see a hole in the ground. She was a beautiful part of that collage herself as the radiance lit her face. Now she understood why everyone called it "Grand."

I stared across that canyon and into the setting sun, arms around my family, feeling like I was finally exactly where I belonged. But I couldn't help but wonder, *Lord, why'd You take me so far out of the way to get where I was going?*

Just wait, God said. *You'll see.*

44

I Really Like You

After a year on the road as a family, we sold the RV and rented an apartment south of Nashville in Carrington Hills. The kids cried as the new owner drove the Thor away. Every chapter of life ends and a new one begins.

The apartment felt even more crowded than the motor home. When you're traveling in an RV, the whole world is your patio. Living in an apartment was a different kind of small.

After a few cramped months, we bought a wood and brick Craftsman in the hills of Franklin, Tennessee. Small yard, no garden. Pool across the street.

I was closer to the music business than I'd ever been, able to cowrite songs with other artists and songwriters on a regular basis. I had written over a hundred songs within the first year and a half of being away from the band, most of them for other artists, but I missed making music of my own.

Slowly, I started digging back into my musical heart and head space, tackling themes of blind faith, trust, and stepping out of comfortable spaces to follow Christ. I wrote about how hard it was to move on from Sanctus Real, standing at the crossroads as seasons change, feeling restless, fighting denial, still feeling guilt over disappointing the band but knowing that I was doing the right thing. I wrote about letting go and embracing the future, accepting that everything doesn't have to look perfect for me to be okay.

Sarah and I continued to release weekly episodes of the *Lead Me Lifecast,* sharing our experiences with a wider audience, unfiltered and totally open about the problems we faced on our path to the marriage we had always wanted.

We weren't experts or teachers, but God was helping us to work out some key issues, and we wanted to invite others into the conversation. We continued to discover what we already knew. Faith, family, and love are messy. That's why we discussed our life in practical terms and stories. Forget the fancy terminology and sermonizing. Jesus used parables to get His point across. We trusted the Spirit and simply let our story speak.

Sarah and I laughed and teased each other on the show. We disagreed. We talked about our tempers and bad habits and all the daily ways we miss the mark. I think I figured out why God often calls the unequipped. You learn a lot by doing. Preparation is great, but there's something to be said for learning to swim by diving into the deep end of the pool.

Telling our story gave us a new perspective, and as we recorded each episode, we reinforced the lessons God had brought us through so far. Don't hide. Don't blame. Practice radical honesty. Pay attention. Listen, don't fix. Trust God for the change.

Women don't want to be fixed. We long to be heard, accepted, known, and validated. Show understanding, accept responsibility, and express love in ways that are meaningful to *me*. We're going to hurt each other in marriage. But as long as I feel free to express my feelings, we can work things out. —Sarah

Can I add a few thoughts from husbands to wives as well?

Please don't expect us to read your mind. Please don't wait until you are nuclear-level furious to unload your deepest thoughts and desires. I know the stress of life can leave us irritable and impatient at times, but beneath our frustrations are crushing insecurities from some secret broken places in our lives.

To win, we need to know that you are for us. On our side. Simple phrases like *I believe in you* are wind in our sails, which so easily fall and tatter. We need to know you won't lose sight of the boy you once knew before life toughened us up. Even through fits of ego and stupidity and consistently leaving the toilet seat up at night, we desperately need your gentle hand to lift us.

At the end of the day, we want to be known and accepted too. To know that through thick and thin and crazy, you are with us and *for* us. You and me, against the world.

I really like you. And I want to spend time with you. I want to do life together. —Sarah

Sarah said that on the *Lifecast* one day. There was so much healing in those few simple words. Our marriage was far from perfect. A lot of things didn't turn out the way we had hoped or planned. But it was uniquely our own, starting that day when I looked across a crowded field and found myself captivated by a barefoot, blue-eyed girl in overalls.

Good times and bad, it was our story. And we weren't finished writing it yet.

45

Back to Where It All Began

My dad shuffled through his dresser drawers. Spare change, Chap-Stick, receipts. But no cufflinks. It was my fault for buying a shirt with french cuffs in the first place. I wore denim jackets and skinny jeans my entire career, so what do I know about putting together business professional attire?

I was back home in Ohio, debating whether I should continue on to our nation's capital for a briefing of faith leaders at the White House. It was an honor to be invited, but some of my colleagues were opting out of the event, fearing career backlash. Has it really come to that point? You can't have lunch and a civil conversation in Washington without making half the country mad? Jesus rose above politics. Shouldn't we aspire to do the same?

"How do you have to dress to be White House appropriate?" I grumbled to my mother. "A vest? Tie bar? Ugh, I don't know if cuff-links are necessary or even still in style."

"Here, go buy some cufflinks, Matthew," Mom said, offering a card for 30 percent off purchases at Kohl's. I reached for the coupon and she pulled it away. "Can I trust you not to lose this? I need it back to buy Christmas presents. You can use these more than once, you know."

"I won't lose your coupon, Mom," I said with a laugh. "Promise."

I grabbed the keys to Dad's 2007 Grand Marquis. White, low miles. Palm Beach edition. He inherited it from my granddad, the one who jumped trains. Maybe it'll get passed down to Bowen one day. I bet the miles on that car will still be less than the number of days it's been off the factory line.

As I drove Dad's old boat toward the Perrysburg Kohl's, my stomach started twisting in knots. It wasn't the DC trip that was making me nervous. It was the trip I was getting ready to take down memory lane at my alma mater, Toledo Christian School.

I was scheduled to return the following day to perform and speak at a TCS fund-raiser. Tuition rarely covers the cost of running a private school. Donors make special projects, building upgrades, and extracurricular programs possible. That weekend it would be my job to share about the positive impact Christian education had on my heart and story in hopes that donors would be generous and help further the legacy of Toledo Christian School.

———

I peered through the windows of my first-grade classroom, hands cupped around my eyes to block the glare. Same turn-handle windows and dusty aluminum blinds. Fourth desk, second row. That was my seat. *Has it really been thirty years?*

I continued down the hall alone, the glow of exit signs lighting my way. I passed my old locker, thinking about the wedgies and noogies and books knocked out of my hands. There was a sign posted over the water fountain, meant to prevent bullying. I hope it helps, but there will always be shy kids who lack the courage to speak up.

I stopped at the south stairwell and peered up through the railing to the third-floor ceiling. When I was in third grade, a kid fell from the top floor all the way to the bottom, breaking his teeth out and spilling a pool of blood on the linoleum below. "He's lucky to be alive," my mother told me.

I ducked into Mom's old office, thinking back to all the days I stared out her window as the other kids ran free at the sound of the last bell. A familiar rattle and hum seeped in from around the corner. I poked my head into the staff kitchen, amazed to see the same old stainless refrigerator. Strange what you remember and what you forget.

The copy room was across the way. Same fridge, new copier. I bet I ran off ten thousand announcement sheets for my mother in that room.

A few steps down the hall stood the tall wooden doors of the chapel. Stained-glass windows, wooden pews. I remembered my last years at TCS, how everything felt so exciting and new. I needed more of that in my life. I didn't want to be one of those people who get jaded and weighed down by life. The Bible says we are always young in God's presence. He is always doing something new.

I thought about my brother's red guitar and the first time I led worship on that chapel stage. I thought about Sanctus Real, before the hits or Nashville, before we got a deal. It felt like Chris should have been there with me, that this should be his homecoming too. And Mark, who braved being the outsider, crashing Wednesday morning chapels to keep the rock and worship alive. Sometimes I missed the band. Closure is difficult to orchestrate. Seemed like we'd left a lot of things unsaid.

What would I say if they were here with me now? I thought. Nothing came to mind except that the depth of the life we shared together can make words seem cheap. Maybe that's why we didn't talk much. Maybe words would've fallen short, somehow making less of what we meant to each other. Maybe it was better left understood. Sometimes there simply are no words.

There was a shortcut I used to take from the chapel to art class, down a creepy back staircase. I walked past the nurse's station, where I would lie on starched white sheets when my stomach was churning from a panic attack. That mystical smell of school took me back through time. Peeling paint and old textbooks, bleach and disinfectants. Dirty mop water, glue sticks, sweaty gym shoes. Fresh pencil shavings and old crayons.

The lunchroom was at the end of the hall. First long table from the door—that's where my last infamous upchuck took place. Ms. Duval told me to clean up a trail of brownie crumbs on the floor, just as a classmate smashed it further into the tile with his shoe. I remember staring at the pile of soggy crumbs, my gag reflex roaring. *How'd a hair get in there?*

I pleaded with her, telling her there'd be a bigger mess if she made me clean it up. But it was Ms. Duval, so I got to work and sure enough . . . bleecchh!

For a moment, I felt ten years old again. The humiliation, all eyes on me. The anxiety and inability to control myself. Had I traveled around the world, singing songs and telling people about Jesus, speaking about what it means to be a man? Was I really married with four children? Did I have a house in Music City? Or was I still a kid dreaming all this up in my cardboard rocket ship?

Shake it off, Matt. The world keeps turning. It's time to perform.

Toledo Christian's chapel band kicked off the evening by leading the crowd in worship. I was surprised so many people were there, considering David Crowder was performing five minutes down the road.

I took the stage when they were done and started into a reimagined version of "Whatever You're Doing (Something Heavenly)," just me and my acoustic. I thought back to when I'd played that song for fifteen people in the middle of nowhere. Back when I wanted nothing more than to lay down my guitar and go home. Now I was home in a sense, back to where it all began. The TCS eagle was in flight on the wall behind me, wings spread, talons reaching, bordered by the school colors of navy and gold.

At the other end of the court, eye level with the stage, bold letters proclaimed Isaiah 40:31. The font was a little smaller, but the weight of those words remained.

> Those who hope in the LORD will renew their strength. They
> will soar on wings like eagles . . .

I finished the verse in my head. *They will run and not grow weary. They will walk and not be faint* (NIV). By the grace of God, I still believe. And here I am, still running the race.

I pulled out a sheet of paper before the final song. "I wrote a little something recently about my days at TCS," I told the students. "Anybody want to hear it?"

"YEAH!" the crowd shouted.

I cleared my throat and began to read. "They called me the Barf King . . ."

Laughter turned to tears as I continued, telling the story of that shy, insecure kid who once walked those same halls, who struggled with bullies and weight gain, who wrote songs about God and started a band and tried to find a place in this world to fit in.

My voice cracked as I read the final words. ". . . and I am so grateful that Mrs. Segler chose anxious me to be her Hero that year."

The students cheered loudly while teachers wiped away tears. I played the opening chords of "Lead Me." Emmy Mae, Claire, Bowen, and Lewis—they were all lingering near the stage. I could see Bowen singing along to every word. My parents and in-laws watched from the second row. Old friends, classmates, and teachers were scattered across the room.

I scanned the crowd, searching. Down the center aisle, I found her. "Lead Me" will always be Sarah's song. For years I sang it with shame. Now it feels hopeful instead. When I sing it these days, I feel a little bit closer to the man I'm supposed to be.

Our marriage will never be perfect. Nothing is perfect in this life. Sarah walked through hell and back with me. But we walked it together. Twenty years later, we are still here, still together, still in love. Grace is amazing; it really is.

I caught her eye, and she smiled that same carefree smile that captured my heart so long ago. We exchanged that look between lovers that goes beyond words. To everyone else she was the cute young mom shooting a quick video of her husband singing at his old high school. But I saw so much more.

I saw the dreams we reimagined coming true. I saw kids and grandkids and growing old together, hand in hand. I saw blue eyes sparkling with life.

A thought struck me as I let the last chord ring.

You know, I should make that girl brownies sometime.

Think About It

1. Boundaries. They're important, whether in a marriage, in a friendship, with extended family—you name it. On a scale of 1 to 5 with 1 being "low" and 5 being "high," how do you score when it comes to both drawing and maintaining boundaries?

2. Trust was broken between Sarah and me. And it had to be rebuilt over time. Consider a time you broke trust with someone or someone broke trust with you. If you need forgiveness, is your ego keeping you from being humble and patient through the process? If you need to forgive, is pride or bitterness standing in your way?

3. Your spouse has God-given intuition and wisdom that you may not have. This can help you make stronger decisions. Has your spouse or a close friend expressed a "gut check" about a relationship or situation that you're in? Have you valued the input or dismissed it?

4. Perhaps it's not you, but someone close to you who is in an unhealthy relationship or situation. How can you be a good friend? Is there some wisdom or advice that you're meant to lovingly communicate? I know it's hard to speak up, but consider the consequences of remaining silent.

5. In the face of neglect, what's beautiful dies and what's ugly thrives. Have you been apathetic, indifferent, or even neglectful when it comes to leading those you love? What do you want the garden of your marriage and family to look like a year from now? In ten years? Fifty? Make a list of what needs to go and what needs to grow in your garden.

6. Is there anything in your life that God is prompting you to change? This could be something major or something minor. But if you are sensing God's nudge to change, what intentional steps are you taking toward making that change? Consider sharing God's prompting with a spouse or trusted friend.

Outro

What will they say when I'm gone, in words that are
written in stone? Under my name, what will they say
about me? I want to leave a legacy to be remembered.

—From "Legacy" by Sanctus Real

A layer of frost was glistening over the hood of my car, slowly dissipating in patches from the heat of the engine. I had my knees tight against the steering wheel because my hands were a little tied up. I realize it's not safe to pilot a Toyota SUV with one's legs, and I'm sure the policeman I passed didn't appreciate it, but I had to capture the moment. I was driving home from a short trip. On a Saturday morning.

I wasn't on a bus somewhere across the desert or driving through snow-capped mountains to a show. I was not going to have to schedule Christmas parties with my wife and kids to fit around a string of concerts. Maybe you can't grasp the importance of being home on a Saturday—and not just home but actually rested—but for me, it had been a dream for many years. So much so that on this holiday morning, I wanted to document every tiny detail.

I parked and walked the steps to my front door. Our Christmas tree was lit, angel on top nearly touching the ceiling. The smell of cookies drifted in from the kitchen.

Emmy was curled up under her favorite blanket, watching *Elf* for the forty-seventh time. Bowen whacked the fire out of his drum kit, while Claire called from her room, trying to get him to lay down his sticks and come play dolls. Hurricane Lewis barreled down the stairs, blazing a trail with his foam sword and fart-blaster gun.

"Hey, babe," said Sarah, greeting me with a kiss. "Welcome home."

The house is a mess, but really, I don't mind. Sarah and I have no agenda for the rest of our lazy Saturday. We might cuddle up and watch Christmas movies or play a family board game. Or we might just sit on the couch and talk. You know, like we did when we were kids. I know now that love can look like a thousand little things that may never be realized until they're gone.

All this may seem ordinary to you, but it's extraordinary to me. And the best part is, this is not the rare exception. Extraordinary Saturdays are the new normal for me.

Bowen just had another birthday, alive and curious and a blessing to us all. He still needs his third-stage repair. But Sarah's "mommy gut feeling" says wait for now. At a recent checkup, the doctor told us that Bowen's heart looks "as good as a single-ventricle can look." So we hold steady, thankful and trusting God for every breath in his blueberry skin.

And me? Well, I've got songs to write. Stories to tell. Books, conferences. My mind stays full of projects all the time. I don't *have* to be creative. I *get* to, because I have boundaries in my life and the space to breathe and enjoy using my gifts in ways that are healthy for me and my family. We're even making a film together, called *Bowen's Heart*.

I've rediscovered what it means to be a dreamer, that same kid holed up in his multicolored cardboard rocket ship. I still deal with anxiety, but with God's help and grace, I'm learning to be courageous. I can finally say I'm a good father, husband, and friend. And I believe *I can* be the man that God has called me to be.

There's a quote that's attributed to Mother Teresa. It's hand painted in a frame hanging on the wall of my home. It says, "If you want to bring happiness to the whole world, go home and love your family." If we all did that more, it would change the world indeed.

What does that look like? Based on where I started out and where I find myself now, I have a few ideas.

Let's take the intentions in our heads and our hearts
Start using our hands to build a home, make a mark.
Schedule time to be together,
Create moments and cultivate laughter.
Read God's Word, teach and learn.
Pray with each other, become better listeners.
Spend quality time, not just talk about it.
Face a hard issue instead of skating around it.
Raise up a family, strengthen our homes,
Create a safe place to be loved and known.
We're just one house, but imagine a world
Where daddies were always there for their girls.
We silenced our phones and shut out the noise
To focus on wrestling through life with our boys,
Leading through actions, not just intentions,
Spiritual servants, emotionally present.
Imagine a world where every child felt loved,
Where wives were never lonely, because they felt understood.
A world where families stayed together,
The fabric of culture grew stronger and better.
Less about me, more about us,
Sacrificially building a home with True Love.

Acknowledgments

My heartfelt thanks to everyone who has played a part, big or small, seen or unseen, in my story. There are a few I'd like to mention by name. Mom and Dad, thank you for modeling true love, character, and genuine faith. Sarah and my children, Emmy, Claire, Bowen, and Lewis, I'm blessed beyond measure to call you mine. Mark and Chris, I'm grateful for the winding road you shared with me, as brothers. Jamie Blaine, thanks for building this house with me. Most of all, thanks to God, the author of life and seasons, who uses my mess as part of His masterpiece.